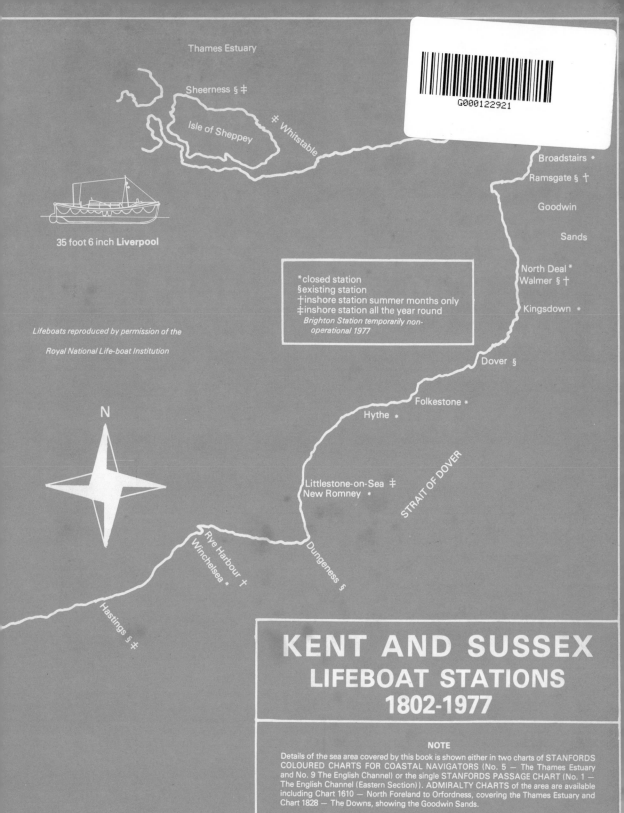

Thames Estuary

Sheerness § ‡

Isle of Sheppey

‡ Whitstable

Broadstairs *

Ramsgate § †

Goodwin

Sands

North Deal *
Walmer § †

Kingsdown *

35 foot 6 inch **Liverpool**

*closed station
§existing station
†inshore station summer months only
‡inshore station all the year round
Brighton Station temporarily non-operational 1977

Lifeboats reproduced by permission of the

Royal National Life-boat Institution

Dover §

Folkestone *

Hythe *

STRAIT OF DOVER

Littlestone-on-Sea ‡
New Romney *

N

Rye Harbour †

Winchelsea *

Dungeness §

Hastings § ‡

KENT AND SUSSEX
LIFEBOAT STATIONS
1802-1977

NOTE

Details of the sea area covered by this book is shown either in two charts of STANFORDS COLOURED CHARTS FOR COASTAL NAVIGATORS (No. 5 — The Thames Estuary and No. 9 The English Channel) or the single STANFORDS PASSAGE CHART (No. 1 — The English Channel (Eastern Section)). ADMIRALTY CHARTS of the area are available including Chart 1610 — North Foreland to Orfordness, covering the Thames Estuary and Chart 1828 — The Downs, showing the Goodwin Sands.

THE SOUND OF MAROONS

Another Terence Dalton Lifeboat Book:

SAVED FROM THE SEA by Robert Malster
The story of Life-Saving Services on the East Anglian Coast.

ISBN 0 900963 32 8

THE SOUND OF MAROONS

The Story of Life-Saving Services on the Kent and Sussex Coasts

by

HOWARD BIGGS

TERENCE DALTON LIMITED

LAVENHAM . SUFFOLK

1977

Published by
TERENCE DALTON LIMITED
ISBN 0 900963 83 2

Text photoset in 11/12pt Baskerville

Printed in Great Britain at
THE LAVENHAM PRESS LIMITED
LAVENHAM . SUFFOLK

Contents

Index of Illustrations

Publishers' Note

Metrication   Throughout this book British measurements have been used and no attempt has been made to change these to metric equivalents. A short list of basic conversions is to be found at the end of the Glossary.

Nautical terms   For the convenience of those unused to these terms a Glossary is appended at the end of the book.

Time   Throughout the measurement of time has been given in a.m. and p.m. No attempt has been made to use the 24-hour clock even after the Admiralty adopted it in 1924.

R.N.L.I.   This abbreviation, for the Royal National Life-boat Institution, has been used throughout although the service did not change to this title until 1854.

Money   Prices prior to decimalisation are given in "old" money. The pound sterling remains unchanged, except in value, but the divisions of the "old" pound are shown at the end of the Glossary.

Introduction and Acknowledgements

FOR centuries the tumbling shallow seas of the English Channel with its formidable sandbanks and reefs have been the familiar haunt of the lugger owners of Margate, Broadstairs, Ramsgate and Deal, and the fishermen from Dover and the Sussex coast. These seafarers of old were dauntless men, true to the best traditions of sailors they would always be ready to risk life and limb to help a brother seaman in danger. Coastguards, hovellers and pilots joined in the great call of saving life long before purpose-built lifeboats were ever employed.

But with Lionel Lukin's testing of the *Experiment* at Ramsgate in 1785 and the *Witch* off the Kent coast soon after there came a new impetus to the saving of life at sea. Boats built by Greathead of South Shields came to Ramsgate in 1802, to Rye and Newhaven in 1803. These were the first of a long list of innovations directly connected with our Kent and Sussex shores. Christopher Wilson of London was granted a medal by the Royal Society of Arts for his "self-balanced" boat at Newhaven; James Peake's improved Beeching design was tested at Brighton, and Tulloch and Boydell's carriage was first supplied to Dungeness where also the prototype extra-light Rubie lifeboats were stationed.

Entering the mechanical era, the first petrol engine was tried out in the *J. McConnel Hussey* of Folkestone at Newhaven, the Newhaven boat itself was fitted with a 24 h.p. Thornycroft and the ex-Ramsgate boat had a 30 h.p. Tylor. Additional experiments with caterpillar tractor launching were at Worthing, while Dover was the pioneer station for fast motor lifeboats. Hastings was the proving-ground for the electric capstan; and, finally, tests with diesel engines led to the boat intended for Selsey being the first to be fitted with twin 40 h.p. diesels.

In this book I have sought to show something of the story behind these seaside towns' links with lifeboat service. Necessarily the accounts have been short for a complete book could easily be written about each individual station, but I hope that, at least, I may have produced a readable book while at the same time giving sufficient technical detail to satisfy the lifeboat historian. Above all I hope that in these pages there may stand out the quality of these longshore fishermen and others who have volunteered to man the boats; for without their quiet devotion, hours of work, which is arduous, and frequently dangerous, our lifeboat service could not operate. Equally, as Bert Goldfinch of Ramsgate once said to me, "If it weren't for you fund-raisers we wouldn't be here". So this book is not only a tribute to these brave men but also to the wonderful enthusiasm and dedication of all Branch officials and Ladies' Guilds for the hours of selfless work they put in to further the cause.

Much has had to be left out, errors may have crept in—for which I must assume responsibility—but there is one particular point I would like to make. In all my researches, enquiries and interviews I have had unfailing help and support from local branches and crews. It has been an inspiration to me to make contact with so many wonderful lifeboat people who have motored miles to meet me, allowed me access to their records and taken endless trouble to help with this work.

It would be impossible to mention them all but I would like to thank, in particular, Grahame Farr for his exhaustive technical and historical information, W. Honey for his invaluable assistance in the maritime history of Deal, Miss Ann Roper, M.B.E., F.S.A. for the *Benvenue* documents, Tony Payne for his generous help, the members of staff at R.N.L.I. Headquarters and the staff of the Public Libraries who have been most helpful. Others without whose aid I could not have embarked on this work include H. Andrews, Mrs Cara Ashley, C. M. Ayling, Alderman C. F. Baker, J.P., R. J. Bloomfield, P. Cheney, H.M. Coastguards, especially Commander R. J. Cardale, M.B.E., R.N. of the Coastguard Training School and Station Officers E. G. Straight, W. F. Carter and E. Fenton; D. D. Cockayne, Jack Froom of the Thames Estuary Research Group, Captain Gibbons, J. C. Harrison, F. S. Hewlett, Arthur Hobby, R. F. Jessup, F.S.A., A. D. Kirkaldie, W. H. Lapthorne, Jeff Morris, G. J. Parkes, E. D. G. Payne, R. K. Sayer, M.B.E., Captain N. B. J. Stapleton, D. Stewart, Mrs Davenport Taylor and Mrs A. E. Turner. And above all my wife who has shared and worked with me in every stage of this book.

Howard Biggs
Broadstairs, Kent.
May, 1977.

Kathleen Mary, a 47 foot × 13 foot Watson at Newhaven.   *A. S. Payne*

CHAPTER ONE

THE THAMES ESTUARY

Sheerness, Whitstable and Margate

THE view from Foreness Point near Margate across the Thames Estuary is striking. Looking north-eastward on a calm summer's day it appears that one is looking over the open sea, for the water stretches away to the far horizon with no trace of land; yet really this is all part of the mouth of a mighty river. Although the seas appear peaceful enough, there is a fringe of foam to the northward marking the Margate Sands, the Tongue lightvessel rears its central tower in the middle distance and every mile of these deceptively innocent blue waters masks a hidden menace. It only needs the study of the chart to realise the perils facing the mariner. From the fang-like ridge of the Longnose, a reef of weed-covered rock stretching straight out from the chalk cliffs, to the innumerable banks of cement-hard sand miles off shore, dangers abound.

In these days powerful freighters or container ships plough through the intricate channels on their way to London docks regardless of weather, skilful pilotage guiding them safely to their destination. But often the giant oil tankers on passage to the Isle of Grain through the Barrow Deep have only a matter of inches of clear water beneath their keels despite the careful dredging undertaken by the Port of London Authority.

Imagine the perils facing seamen in the days of sail when a foul slant of wind could set a vessel onto the Knock John or the Long Sand in a matter of minutes; when missing stays or gear carrying away in a gale could spell disaster on the Barrow or the Shingles.

Similar dangers abound on the northern side of the Estuary where the great extent of the Maplins fringe the bankstrewn waters. Off this remote part of Essex where once the only road to Foulness and its scattered farmsteads was by the ancient broomway over the sands, collier brigs from Newcastle brought cargoes of coal to London running south-west through the Wallet, while Onker brigs came from Scandinavia with timber. From Tudor times hoys and luggers worked right up into the creeks to load corn or other produce direct from the farm. Today, the rotting remains of wharves far up the creeks and inlets are silent reminders of the cargoes carried across the Estuary to the mills at Sittingbourne or Faversham. Sir Francis Drake is reputed to have learnt the rudiments of seamanship aboard a hoy—the forerunners of the splendid Thames barges whose tanned mains'ls were a common sight around the south east coast earlier this century.

It was natural therefore that seamen on both the northern and southern shores of the Estuary were alert to help ships in distress, especially the longshore fishermen whose knowledge of the banks and skill in handling their own shallow-draught

Naming of *Canadian Pacific* (ON 803) 30th May, 1939.　　　*Central Press Photos.*　*R.N.L.I.*

vessels made them all the more ready to give effective help to those in danger. In a description of Margate, for example, published in 1820, four years before the Royal National Life-boat Institution was founded, reference was made to the foreshore east of the pier. In Oulton's *Picture of Margate* the writer stated, "Here boats are always kept ready for launching at all times in case of distress, and to the great credit of Margate sailors it must be acknowledged that they have never been backward in lending their assistance in the worst of weather."

With the coming of steam the brigs were replaced by steam colliers able to keep at sea and bring fuel to the capital in all weathers, the great East Indiamen and square-riggers gave way to the early steam-and-sail liners, but all this while the small coasters clung to sail, hoys adapted as small passenger craft made the trip from London to Southend and Margate as these coastal resorts grew in importance.

With more and more ships using the Port of London and its growth as the principal mercantile centre of the country it is appropriate that the inaugural meeting of the Royal National Life-boat Institution—then known as the National Institution for the Preservation of Life from Shipwreck—should have taken place in the City. On the initiative of Thomas Wilson, M.P. for the City of London, many notable people assembled on 4th March, 1824, at the *City of London Tavern,* presided over by the Archbishop of Canterbury, Dr Manners Sutton. Among those present were the Bishops of London and Chester, William Wilberforce of anti-slave trade fame, Captain Manby, well-known for his experiments with line-throwing mortars, and many others, all gathered as a result of the detailed and stimulating pamphlet* produced by Sir William Hillary the previous year. Most appropriately, too, the first headquarters of the Institution were at 12 Austin Friars in the City; and the City was still the centre from which its work was directed until 1851.

The National Institution for the Preservation of Life from Shipwreck thus formed was soon granted the prefix "Royal" by King George IV, who consented to become its patron. Lord Liverpool, the Prime Minister, became its President, five Royal Dukes were Vice-Presidents, while technical help was given by men of such wide experience as Captain John Foulerton, an Elder Brother of Trinity House, and Captain Saumarez R.N., the latter even taking the Brighton lifeboat in 1828 out on trials in heavy seas to test its performance. But above all the Institution owed its successful inception to Sir William Hillary, who not only laid down the principles for its formation, but was himself a practical lifeboatman assisting in saving over 300 lives.

The Kent and Sussex stations have connections with the earliest years of the Institution as may be seen from the mention of the Brighton lifeboat; but their links with life-saving go back far beyond its foundation. It was to Ramsgate, for example, that one of the first boats adapted as a lifeboat was sent by Lionel Lukin for testing in 1785. Lukin who was by profession a coach-builder in London had been born at Dunmow in Essex, and his other great interest was in perfecting what he described as an "unimmergible boat", a model of which he tested on the "Doctor's Pond" at Dunmow. Encouraged by the interest shown by one of his customers, the Prince of

An appeal to the British Nation on the Humanity and Policy of Forming a National Institution for the Preservation of Lives and Property from Shipwreck.

Memorial statue on Margate sea-front to the 9 crew of the surf-boat *Friend to all Nations* who lost their lives when she capsized on 2nd December, 1897. Mr Troughton of the Margate Ambulance Corps was the 10th casualty.
R.N.L.I.

Wales (later George IV), he bought a Norwegian yawl, added a cork gunwale, air cases fore and aft and along the thwarts, and an additional iron plate to the keel to provide greater strength and stability. He patented his ideas in 1785 and sent the boat, named the *Experiment*, to be tested by a Ramsgate pilot. The tests proved the boat to be beyond all that had been expected, for when high winds and heavy seas forced all other craft into shelter the *Experiment* would put out into the channel and return safely after a stormy trip. However it was not long before rumours began to circulate about the activities of this boat, the local preventive men became interested and kept watch, and before long she was seized, confiscated and destroyed after her skipper was found guilty of carrying cargoes of contraband. But, Lukin, never a man to be deflected by a little smuggling, built a further boat on similar lines which he named the *Witch* and tested in the roughest weather off the Kent coast. Learning of his experiments Archdeacon Sharp, the administrator of the Crewe Trust, commissioned him to adapt a Northumbrian coble for use as a lifeboat at Bamburgh. This he did, and the boat was in service by 1787.

Lukin has another close connection with the history of the Kent lifeboats as he later lived at Hythe in Kent. His interest in lifeboats remained very keen and it was he who first realised the need for using different types of boat on different coasts. He wrote, "It is particularly advisable that all lifeboats should be built of the form most approved by the pilots and seamen of the coast where they are to be used; as no one form will fit all shores." He lived to see the formation of the Institution to whose work his inventions made such a contribution, and when he died in 1834 these words were inscribed on his tombstone in Hythe churchyard, "This Lionel Lukin was the first who built a lifeboat and was the original inventor of that principle of safety by which many lives and much property have been preserved from shipwreck. . ."

All of the Thames Estuary and south east coast ports have long histories of seafaring or, in the case of Sheerness, of dockyard work. From Tudor times, when the Royal Navy was first established as a regular Service to replace the Cinque Ports fleet which was only called upon in time of war, Sheerness held a key position as a coastal defence centre. The Dutch attack of 1667 aroused such public outcry that the Admiralty decided to build a dockyard there. Gradually it was extended but the Napoleonic wars overtaxed its resources to such an extent that in 1813 John Rennie was directed to plan a new dockyard complex. He and his son supervised the construction of this fine yard, a great basin 63 feet wide at the entrance and with 3 dry docks, the whole built upon foundations of soft mud and loose quicksands, an astonishing example of skilful engineering and originality.

Also Sheerness, Chatham and Gillingham Reaches were the mooring places for many of the prison hulks which housed both prisoners of war and convicted

The first Station lifeboat at Sheerness, the *Gertrude*, a typical 46 foot × 12 foot 9 inch Watson, built in 1946.   *R.N.L.I.*

criminals at the beginning of the nineteenth century. With as many as 30,000 French prisoners in 1798 shore quarters were hopelessly overstrained. Some were kept in unusual places such as the Margate caves and many were confined on partly unrigged battleships aboard which conditions were harsh and punishments severe. By 1856 the last of the hulks were scrapped and just a century later, under post-war rationalisation, the naval dockyard was closed, the site being developed partly as an industrial area, partly as a ferry terminal and deep water harbour. It was here that the R.N.L.I. Committee of Management considered establishing a new lifeboat station in 1969.

In the post-war years life-saving has been very greatly influenced by the development of the helicopter, the Thames Estuary and the Kent and Sussex coasts being covered principally by the R.A.F. rescue helicopters at Manston and, in the immediate post-war years, by the U.S.A.F. also stationed at the same airfield. Ironically it was the withdrawal of the R.A.F. helicopters that was one of the major considerations in establishing the Sheerness station. A vigorous outcry among the inhabitants of the seaside towns and many yachtsmen, including Mr Edward Heath, resulted in a commercial firm being entrusted with the provision of helicopter coverage; but there were also other problems facing the rescue services. With the fall-off in pleasure steamer traffic from London to the coast, Southend pier, in common with so many others, faced a drop in revenue; a survey reported a need for large scale expenditure to maintain the safety of ironwork and deck. The serious fire of 1976 has emphasised the problem. This was a grave matter for the longest pier in the United Kingdom, and serious, too, for the lifeboat station at the seaward end of it. Therefore it was decided to try out an alternative station on the southern shore at Sheerness.

The *Ernest William and Elizabeth Ellen Hinde,* ON 1017, a 40 foot lifeboat built in G.R.P.* was sent here on evaluation trials, both to give further test to the potentialities of this new building material in lifeboat construction and to discover what demand there was for a station. From the number of calls it soon became obvious that the need existed and in 1971 the decision to establish a permanent station was confirmed. ON 1017 remained until the end of 1969 during which spell 32 calls were received and since that date Sheerness has become one of the busiest lifeboat stations on the south east coast. Up till March 1975 there were 165 calls resulting in the saving of 137 lives which affords ample proof of the value of this new station.

Between 1970 and 1974 an older lifeboat, the *Gertrude,* ON 847, a 46 foot × 12 foot 9 inches Watson design craft of 20 tons, did duty here, Coxswain Charles Bowry and his crew finding her a splendid boat. She was built in 1946, re-engined with Parsons Barracuda Diesels in 1966 and had at first been station boat at Holy Island. Assisted for a time by the *William Taylor of Oldham,* ON 917, another Watson, previously at Coverack, she remained until their new and much faster 44 foot Waveney class the *Helen Turnbull,* ON 1027, was delivered in 1974. Both coxswain and crew have grown very attached to her, and it was in this boat that

*Glass Reinforced Plastic.

Charles Bowry carried out a noteworthy service* in the early morning of the 16th August, 1975, to the 30 foot yacht *Eladnid* which was hard and fast on the West Barrow Sands.

She was lying on her port bilge with waves breaking over her stern, in a very confused and rough sea, and there was only about a foot of water over the bank at that stage of the tide. As he worked in as close as he could to the northward of the yacht the coxswain found that the *Helen Turnbull* was rolling wildly in her position athwart wind and tide so that rescue work could not be attempted. The lifeboat moved to the windward, anchored, and veered down toward the casualty. A man could be seen clinging to the cabin top but obviously in no position to tend a line, so the coxswain decided to veer the lifeboat's inflatable dinghy down to the yacht with two of his own crew aboard. At the second attempt, despite being filled over and over again by seas, the inflatable reached the yacht and the two crew members scrambled aboard. They found there were three adults in all, two of whom were incapacitated through sea-sickness, and two children aged twelve and eight. Under these circumstances the coxswain having decided not to risk dragging the survivors through the surf by breeches-buoy or in the inflatable, tried to tow the yacht clear. Directing his men to batten everything down, he began to take the strain on a westerly heading to prevent the yacht, which was shipping water heavily, being overturned. By about 3.10 a.m. she was clear of the bank, the coxswain moved cautiously into deeper water and then waited his chance to take the survivors off. Some thirty-five minutes later there was a slight lull, the lifeboat slid rapidly astern and came alongside the yacht and the five were transhipped from yacht to lifeboat, and efforts were made to tow the *Eladnid* to safety. This tow was successful and at 5.45 a.m. they reached the safety of the Sheerness Great Basin. The bronze medal for gallantry was awarded to the coxswain and medal service certificates to members of the crew for this outstanding feat of skilful seamanship.

The next harbour along the North Kent coast is Whitstable, for Faversham, Sittingbourne and Conyer are only reached by creeks and the shipping along the coast keeps well outside the Isle of Sheppey. Even Whitstable itself is still within the Swale, Sheppey looms clear to the north and the amount of shipping is relatively small and limited to coastal and short sea vessels despite boat-building yards and a long history of oyster-dredging. However with more and more people taking to the water for recreation and the great influx of summer visitors this was clearly a place to require rescue coverage. Therefore an I.L.B.† was stationed there in 1963, operational only during the summer months, which has proved of great value, having been launched in the first twelve years 353 times and rescued 145 lives.

In 1968 the Whitstable I.L.B. went out to help the well-known television personality Raymond Baxter. His 30 foot boat was under tow by a friend's yacht en route for Queensborough when the towing craft went aground in the darkness. Both boats dropped anchor but when the wind freshened distress flares were burnt. Very soon the I.L.B., under Fred Downs, was at the scene. Mr Baxter wrote: "One expects R.N.L.I. lifeboatmen to be brave and efficient. What impressed me so

*The setting out of a lifeboat to answer a distress call is known as "a service".
†Inshore Lifeboat.

Whitstable. Small boats at moorings and the Inshore Lifeboat under way.   *R.N.L.I.*

much was that they were also kind. After a short conference it was agreed that they would escort us into Whitstable which was exactly what we required. . . About an hour later we were in Whitstable harbour. What made my day was that they said we had done the right thing in calling for assistance. Just another very minor incident. There was no heroism, no immediate danger, no injury and a broken stanchion on my boat was the only damage sustained—but the I.L.B. was the only craft which could have reached us, she had never operated at night before, she was perfect for the job, and her crew could not have behaved in a more admirable manner."

Situated at the southern extremity of the Thames Estuary some 20 miles further east than Southend, Margate and the North Foreland are passed by all the shipping moving in and out of London and down Channel.

Historically the town is of considerable interest for as a "limb" of Dover it provided 15 ships for the Cinque Ports navy at the siege of Calais in 1347. From then on it was principally a fishing and farming community variously known as Meregate or St John's until, in the seventeenth and eighteenth centuries, it became a favourite port for communication with the Continent, and used as such by George I and George II, by Marlborough and Admiral Duncan and where the wounded and the prisoners from the battle of Waterloo were landed. Because of its importance a

17

wooden jetty was there in 1753 and a strong stone pier built some few years later, to provide a safe landing place and to shelter the local fishing boats and the ship-building yards which specialised in the building of hoys and luggers. Several well-known Thanet names appear among the ship-builders, such as William Gore, Wastall, Huggett, Allan and Farleigh; and the Margate luggers became famous as excellent sea-boats able to sail close to the wind.

With the increasing popularity of sea bathing, more and more people came flocking to Margate. The Quaker Benjamin Beale invented his bathing machine in 1753, the Royal Sea Bathing Hospital was founded in 1791; but still stagecoaches were the main means of transport to the coast. In this situation the hoys, which had been the principal corn and cargo carriers between Essex, Kent and London for many years, provided an excellent alternative. Portions of the hold were re-designed as cabins, and travellers were offered fresh sea-breezes in place of the dust of the highway, all at a cost of 2/6d for the entire trip. The hoy *Margate* in 1802, for example, carried 28 passengers, a crew of four and a load of corn for London. A letter to a Miss Rebecca Prall in 1811 quoted by James Bird in his *Story of Broadstairs and St Peter's* gives an entertaining description of travel by hoy:

"It is a humorous enough scene to go from London to Margate by the hoy. These vessels when you see them lying snug in the harbour appear to be the most comfortable of the kind you can conceive, fitted in such a style of neatness with every attention to convenience that almost astonishes you. When we had got our fair stock of ladies, consisting of tradesmen's wives and daughters and many other people who had a little money to spend we set sail. In about one hour it was announced that ye kettle boiled. To my great astonishment they began to spread their tea and sugar, bread and butter etc on the table as if they had been sitting in their parlour. . . We were on the water 27 hours. When we arrived at the Hope, considerably below Gravesend, the effect of the motion of the vessel was felt by the greater part of our female companions; there did not seem to be that inclination for eating as heretofore. By the time we got into the Channel hardly a person on board was in good health. By the time we arrived at Margate we presented such a figure as I can hardly delineate."

It was the skippers and hands of such hoys, the fishermen and lugger crews whose resourcefulness and skill led to the reference to Margate sailors quoted earlier. Their reputation was amply justified as may be seen from the rescues from the East Indiaman *Hindustan* on 11th January, 1803. In a hard easterly gale, outward bound, she anchored in the Queen's Channel near the Wedge Sand but after two days of storm the anchors dragged and she went ashore. Everything possible was done to save the ship, the mainmast was cut away, a raft constructed but it fouled in the spars and rigging overside, whereupon distress guns were fired and flares burnt. One of the Margate luggers, the *Lord Nelson*, put out manned by John Brothers, her owner, and 16 men; and by the most strenuous exertions they managed to save 129 out of a total complement of 143. Even these luggers manned

Lifeboat *Quiver No. I* returning to Margate after a service.
Drawn by R. P. Leitch. Margate Library

by experienced and skilful seamen could not always launch off. This happened when the *Royal Adelaide*, an Irish packet on her run between Cork and London, went on the Tongue Sands on 6th April, 1850 and 250 lives were lost. This so stirred the Margate boatmen that they determined to purchase the best possible purpose-built lifeboat. On hearing of the good work done by the Broadstairs lifeboat *Mary White*, an order was placed with her builders, J. Samuel White of Cowes.

Aided by local subscriptions the boatmen purchased this White lifeboat themselves while a second lifeboat was bought and presented to the town by Miss (later Baroness) Burdett Coutts. A committee of boatmen and townspeople was formed to manage the boats and the R.N.L.I. congratulated them on setting up their own private organisation, giving them a full set of life-jackets. There seems to be some uncertainty about the services and management of these boats, for the Town Council asked the R.N.L.I. to inspect the Coutts donated boat in 1859, and to take over the station. This was done in 1860, the Coutts boat — possibly named *Hannah and Angela* — being altered to Peake's design by Forrestt of Limehouse.

Thus she became the first R.N.L.I. boat on station at Margate and during her six years of service nine lives were saved. The *Hannah and Angela* was launched from a carriage or dray which was dragged by horses across the sands. A rather similar method was used for the boatmen's boat *Friend of all Nations* which was kept in the harbour or launched off the beach.

In 1866 the pulling and sailing lifeboat *Quiver No 1,* a far more weatherly and efficient boat based upon the design of James Beeching of Great Yarmouth as adapted by Peake, replaced the Coutts boat. Air cases at bow and stern gave her a self-righting capacity, she was 34 foot × 8 foot 3 inches carrying a crew of 13, with oars and lugsails. She was built for the R.N.L.I. by Forrestt of Limehouse as the gift of the *Quiver Magazine* Lifeboat Fund. It was in this boat that the first medal was won by Margate men when, in 1871, the silver medal was awarded to Coxswain William Grant for his rescue of the crew of six of the brig *Sarah* of Sunderland which had been wrecked on the Margate Sands.

Two other extremely arduous services were on the 18th and 20th March, 1873 when the *Quiver* and her gallant crew were at sea for over seven hours on each occasion, rescuing seven people from the brig *Demetrius* of Sunderland and 12 from the Norwegian barque *Noordstar*, both aground on the Long Sand right out in the Estuary. It was bitterly cold on each occasion, with a north-easterly gale requiring a beat of well over 10 miles in a confused sea. The private lifeboat *Friend of all Nations* was also launched for the latter wreck as is recorded in the R.N.L.I. Journal.

Both these boats were pressed into service again in the fateful winter of 1877 when Keeble's *Gazette* 1st December, recorded in the editorial, "So dreadful a gale has not visited this coast since 1808 when the old pier was utterly destroyed". Altogether 25 vessels drove ashore off Margate, eight of them on the Nayland Rock where they lay "pounded by the breakers, with rudders and keels torn away, bulwarks stove in and remnants of their ragged sails tearing away from the yards".

At about 7.30 p.m. on the previous Saturday the *Quiver No 1* was called out in response to signals from a ship in Margate Roads. She was hauled about two miles eastward by the horses and launched off at the Long Nose from which point she could drive in the direction of the distressed ship, the barque *Hero* of Shields. Her main anchor cable had parted and she was dragging her second anchor amid the broken seas at the edge of the Margate Sands. With the greatest difficulty the lifeboat veered alongside, rescuing the crew of 15 men shortly before the second cable gave and the ship finally went ashore off Brook's End, Birchington. The lifeboat next made for another vessel burning flares, the schooner *Louisa* bound for Weymouth with coal. It was clear that if she continued to drive as she was, quite out of control, she would pile up on shore; so two of the lifeboat's crew were put aboard and, piloted by the *Quiver*, they helped to work her into the safety of Whitstable harbour, by about 4 a.m. Sunday morning. The wind by then had risen to hurricane force making it quite impossible for the lifeboat to beat back to her station so the coxswain put her ashore where she could be hauled back by carriage. Several hours later a shift of wind allowed her to put to sea again, and to reach Margate at 3.30 p.m. that afternoon. In the crew on this occasion with Coxswain Grant were Second Coxswain J. Fox, J. Davies, G. Sandwell, J. Sandwell, E. Brett, H. Brockman, S. Ladd, J. Dyke, E. Parker, J. Dixon and T. Campanay; family names that were to recur many times in the story of the Margate lifeboats.

Margate jetty, showing east and west slipways, ships of the Royal Navy in the background, a paddle-steamer just leaving the landing-stage. (c. 1904)   *Margate Library*

When the *Quiver* was launched other vessels were going adrift and in difficulties so the lugger *Enterprise* put to sea under her skipper E. Emptage. They put men aboard the schooner *Commodore* which they assisted into Whitstable, another of the crew assisted the *Erissa* of Guernsey into Dover with the lugger and another schooner, which had lost both her anchors, following astern. Again the names of Parker and Campanay were mentioned, this time among the lugger's crew.

At about 8 p.m. the same night the *Friend of all Nations* put out from the beach near the jetty but after a two hour struggle was driven back into the harbour with the boat full of water. However, putting off again, the crew managed to rescue all eight hands from a fishing smack. Shortly afterwards, with the storm increasing, they made for a brig, the *Julie Estelle* of Cherbourg, in distress and the coxswain was washed overboard but was picked up again. After landing her crew of seven they put out again, left some men to help the schooner *Florence Nightingale* and landed seven from the brig *Quebec*. By this time the tide was falling and the *Friend of all Nations* was left secured in the harbour; but when she was later examined it was found that the air cases at bow and stern were full of water and only the cork round the gunwales rendered her buoyant. It was in this state that a fresh crew endeavoured to take her out on Sunday morning to try to rescue the crew of the schooner *Jane Cameron* but time and again they were beaten back. In the end the Ramsgate tug *Aid* appeared with Ramsgate and Broadstairs lifeboats in tow and the survivors were successfully picked up from the rigging of the stricken vessel. Again many family names such as Ladd, Emptage, Sandwell, Brockman, Brett and Epps are to be found among those who so gallantly manned the surf-boat*. The *Friend of all Nations* was so severely damaged that she had to be scrapped but at least she had saved 31 men in the course of this one gale, and is credited with a total of 80 in her years of service. The boatmen and many of the local people who had witnessed their heroic efforts off the beach were anxious to have another private boat so Mr T. Grey of Birchington provided them with a more weatherly and serviceable boat, the *Friend to all Nations*.

In all that storm, with so many vessels lost and even the iron jetty cut in two by the pounding wreckage from a ship that had been severely damaged three weeks before, not a single life was lost.

This, however, was not the case during the even more severe storm that struck the north-east coast of Kent in November/December 1897. In the intervening years *Quiver No 1* was withdrawn having saved 70 lives and a second *Quiver,* ON 265, a 37 foot × 9 foot self-righter built by Woolfe of Shadwell, came on station. By the time she was withdrawn in 1898 she was credited with saving 61 lives, a figure exceeded by the *Friend to all Nations*. Although as was only natural, there was a certain rivalry between the two boats, the crews were largely interchangeable, with the additional advantage afforded to the surf-boat men that they were not compelled to wear life-jackets which they found hampered their work at the oars.

On Monday, 30th November, 1897, the north north-west wind rapidly increased during the night until it reached hurricane proportions. This continued

*Surf-boat is the term applied to private boats of local design.

Margate lifeboat *Eliza Harriet* launching.
From an old postcard

throughout the next day with the result that the tide built up—rather as in 1953—and waves broke clean over Margate sea front causing extensive damage. The deck of the jetty was broken up, volumes of water pounded against and flowed over the stone pier with waves frequently breaking higher than the lighthouse at the end of it. Cliff protection works were demolished, concert halls, baths and the Marine Pavilion were wrecked, the total damage being estimated at over £5,000. In the dying years of the nineteenth century this was a vast amount of money.

Amid all this the *Friend to all Nations* was launched to assist a ketch seen to be in difficulties off Birchington. She could not be launched from Margate beach but was instead hauled to Birchington by road and launched from there, successfully saving the three men of the crew and their dog.

Meanwhile the R.N.L.I. Honorary Secretary had received reports about further vessels in danger off Westgate. The *Quiver* was drawn along there on her carriage and launched in West Bay, some posts beside the slip having to be chopped away to allow the passage of this larger boat and her trolley. The coxswain, Albert Emptage of the famous lugger-owning family, is reported as saying that "never had he experienced a rougher day or a worse sea". As soon as they were clear of the shore they made for the Hook Sands where they found three barges in distress. Getting alongside the first, the *Flower of Essex*, with some difficulty owing to the tremendous sea running they rescued three men and two dogs, then beat to windward in blinding spray and foam to pick up the crews from the *Lord Beresford*, the *Eustace* of Rochester and the *Enterprise* from Harwich. Altogether they saved 14 hands and three dogs with which load they worked back into Margate with a double reef in their storm sail.

After moderating slightly, just long enough for these barges to be salved and brought safely into harbour, the wind increased again, this time from the northeast and by Thursday was blowing very hard. Early in the morning there came a report that a ship was burning distress flares on the far side of the Margate Sands. She was found later to be the *Persian Empire* which had been damaged in collision with a steamer. At once the *Friend to all Nations* was launched, followed 10 minutes later by the *Quiver*, but very shortly afterwards the surf-boat was struck by a heavy sea and capsized, only four of her crew of 14 being saved. A report of this tragic event refers to it as the first catastrophe to strike Margate for forty-one years — since the lugger *Victory* was lost with nine hands off Kingsgate in 1857. Exactly how the accident happened will probably never be known but one of the survivors stated that the sail was being lowered when a sudden squall took them aback, filled the bellying sail with solid water and thus caused them to go over. Three men, Robert Ladd, Henry Brockman and J. Gilbert, were washed ashore with the boat, the fourth, J. Epps, was found pinioned under the capsized hull and though apparently drowned was eventually resuscitated. At once a fund was started for the relatives and dependants of those who died; a statue of a lifeboatman on Margate sea-front commemorates the death of these brave men. The *Quiver* meanwhile carried out the mission to the *Persian Empire* successfully through very heavy seas.

In spite of this disaster the boatmen still felt the need for a private boat so a second *Friend to all Nations* was built. She was still kept in the harbour, and was converted to motor in 1922. Laid up between 1928 and 1939 she was ordered by the Admiralty to be duty lifeboat for the Thames Estuary when all the others were at Dunkirk, was then requisitioned and used as a Trot boat at Falmouth before being finally sold to a Dutchman who used her as a house-boat; but when her owner attempted to sail her across to Holland she foundered in a sudden squall.

With the increasing use of steam the types of service were changing fast and the internal combustion engine was only a few years away. The rail links between London and the Thanet towns had done away with the hoys but a new form of sea travel had assumed popularity, with *La Marguerite*, the *Royal Sovereign*, *London Belle* and *Eagle* thrashing their paddles down the Estuary on their way to Margate. The launching of the lifeboat from a carriage drawn by horses seemed no longer reasonable and instead slipways were constructed on east and west sides of the jetty. Two boats, 40 foot × 10 foot 6 inches, carrying crews of 15 were built by Roberts of Mevagissey, the *Eliza Harriet*, ON 411, being kept at the head of the West slip, and *Civil Service No 1*, ON 415, on the East.* These two boats did tremendous service, saving over 350 lives between them, the *Eliza Harriet* being involved in a most dangerous rescue from the ketch *Malvoisin* of London. She was from Gravelines bound for Goole with a cargo of phosphates and went ashore on the Kentish Knock in a whole south-east gale. It was the 15th January, 1905, and bitterly cold, the ship had lost her rudder, the sails had blown away and the bulwarks were smashed. In the breaking seas the lifeboat was damaged as she surged alongside. Of the four crew rescued two were in a state of collapse. Second Coxswain S. Clayson was

*Owing to the unsafe state of Margate jetty today the new Rother Class lifeboat, the *Silver Jubilee,* due to come on to the Station in 1978, will be launched by tractor and carriage.

awarded the silver medal for this service and shortly afterward was appointed coxswain, a post he retained until 1926, to make him the last of the Margate sailing lifeboat coxswains. In his twenty-seven years as an officer of the boat he had helped to rescue 367 lives.

After Stephen Clayson retired, Alf Jones held the post for four years until Ted Parker was appointed in 1930. His brother Harry was also a member of the crew whilst Ted was coxswain, and Ted's son was second coxswain for many years under Denis "Sinbad" Price who took over in 1946. Ted Parker was coxswain when the Margate boat took part in the historic evacuation from Dunkirk, the D.S.M. awarded to him being a recognition of the outstanding gallantry of the entire Margate crew in rescuing 600 men from those open beaches. Just as these coxswains have held their positions for very many years, the same has been true of the motor mechanics, Ted Jordan who was mechanic of the first motor lifeboat here, the *Lord Southborough*, being succeeded by Alf Lacey in 1946. His young brother David is also a member of the crew.

The increasing operation range made possible by the use of the motor, meant the Number 1 station was closed in 1937, and the *Lord Southborough*, ON 688, a Watson cabin lifeboat, 45 foot × 12 foot 6 inches, weighing about 20 tons and built by S. E. Saunders of Cowes was housed in the eastern boat-house. In her twenty-six years on station she was launched on service no less than 278 times, rescuing 269 lives excluding the Dunkirk evacuation. However the present boat *North Foreland, Civil Service No 11*, ON 888, has seen some of the most memorable services in Margate's long history. She was built in 1951 by a firm, J. Samuel White of Cowes, whose founder was born at Broadstairs, a 46 foot 9 inches Watson design with a

Stephen Clayson, the last of the pulling and sailing coxswains, alongside the first motor lifeboat at Margate, *Lord Southborough*, in 1927.   *R.N.L.I.*

Denis (Sinbad) Price, Coxswain 1946-1965.
R.N.L.I.

Naming of the *North Foreland* (*Civil Service No. 11*) 1951. *Author's collection*

beam of 12 foot 9 inches, equipped with radar, radio-telephone communication and powered by twin 40 h.p. diesels. On 2nd September that year Alfred Wilson risked his life in the early hours of the morning in boarding the yacht *Girlanda*, which was pitching and rolling violently in the breakers rebounding from the harbour wall, and securing a hawser so that she could be towed to safety. He was clinging to the foredeck with seas sweeping over him for much of the time; for this courageous service he won the bronze medal, also the Maud Smith award for the bravest act of life-saving that year.

Less than a year after her arrival on station, on 18th January, 1952, she was involved in a typically long and arduous service. A fresh north-westerly gale was blowing, with very rough sea and blinding snow squalls when a call was received at half past one in the morning. Within a few minutes the cable was slipped, the boat tore down the slipway and she and her crew had started to battle their way far out into the Thames Estuary, to a position 29 miles east north-east of the North Foreland where the 4-masted barque *Pamir*, then used by the West Germans as a cadet training ship, was making very heavy weather of it. Whilst on her way the lifeboat received a message from the *Pamir's* captain asking her to take off 49 boys. However so dark was the night, so thick the snow squalls that it was not until well after daybreak that the barque was sighted. By then the captain had decided to keep the boys aboard so the *North Foreland* stood by, circling round and round. It was a dramatic meeting between an old square-rigger, a type so often assisted by the old pulling and sailing lifeboats, and a modern diesel-driven Watson. By about 3.30 p.m. a tug arrived, but the seas were so heavy that it was impossible to pass a tow-rope. However at 6.15 p.m. the coxswain saw the *Pamir* start to move and closed with her, thinking the anchor cable might have parted. Lifeboat and tug chased the *Pamir* in the darkness until, with the aid of his searchlight, the coxswain saw that the ship had set storm canvas and was resuming her voyage; whereupon he put into Ramsgate, the nearest port, having been out in heavy snow showers and a full gale for 22 hours. The captain of the *Pamir* sent a message thanking them for standing by.

On this occasion the crew faced discomfort and danger for many hours without having to undertake any actual rescue work. Many calls are like that, a fact that has to be taken into account when examining service records. But on 6th November of the same year a call came which resulted in an even longer trip and a successful rescue.

A whole gale was blowing from the north-west, with gusts up to 80 m.p.h., when at a quarter to three in the morning the Coastguard reported a message from the Mid-Barrow lightvessel the other side of the Estuary. They had sighted red flares to the west of them, but all other lifeboats in the area were already out on service. It was just about high water at Margate and waves were pounding the sea-front and lashing right up to the doors of the boat-house. Nevertheless a crew was quickly assembled and at 3.10 a.m. the *North Foreland* launched and set off on her 20 mile journey across the Estuary. The gale was against her, and it was difficult to see in the squalls of rain, sleet and driving spray. Later Coxswain Price said, "It was one of the worst trips we have ever had." In spite of this, by 6 a.m. the lifeboat was searching along the West Barrow Sands. As day dawned the coxswain saw the mast of a sunken barge, *Vera*, and standing on the headrope of the mainsail two men clinging to the halyards. All around were breaking seas. He knew these men must be exhausted and that there was no time to be lost, so he decided to take the lifeboat right up onto the barge's deck alongside the mast so that they might slide down into her. He had to come in three times because of the heavy seas before both men could be rescued, one of them being so numbed with cold that he almost slid into the water. However the lifeboat crew managed to grab him and haul him to safety. Because of their chilled and exhausted condition after five hours in the rigging, the coxswain decided to put them ashore as quickly as possible so, driving further up the Essex coast, he put in at Brightlingsea, 43 miles from home. Not until later the following day did the *North Foreland* and her crew get back to their station.

For this service the silver medal was awarded to Coxswain Denis Price and special inscriptions of thanks to Second Coxswain Parker and Alfred Lacey, the motor mechanic.

Since then Alf Manning, who saw war service in minesweepers, has taken over as coxswain from Denis Price. The pattern of rescues has been changing with the decline in the coasting trade and alteration in the type of shipping using London docks. Above all there has been a vast increase in services to yachtsmen and small boats, so in 1966 an Inshore Lifeboat was also stationed here. Manning's two sons, Leslie and Peter, were in the crew of this boat since its inception. Already the I.L.B. has proved its worth by having saved well over 100 lives; while in the hundred and sixteen years since the R.N.L.I. took over the Margate station, no less than 1,315 lives have been saved or landed, excluding those rescued by the surf-boat, and five silver and one bronze medal awarded for gallantry.

The work of the lifeboatmen is backed up by the enthusiastic fund raising of Branch and Ladies Lifeboat Guild which cover the cost of maintaining the station and is sufficient also to send a handsome annual donation to the funds of the R.N.L.I.

Margate lifeboat *North Foreland* (*Civil Service No. 11*) standing by the training ship *Pamir* in a gale, 16th January, 1952.   *R.N.L.I.*

CHAPTER TWO

NORTH FORELAND TO
NORTH SAND HEAD

Kingsgate, Broadstairs and Ramsgate

I N THE 1850s and 1860s many of the Coastguard Stations around the south coast were supplied with lifeboats built by J. Samuel White of Cowes. One of these was at Newgate, supplementing the life-saving work of the Margate boatmen. Some two miles further eastward is Kingsgate, with the Longnose Ridge stretching several miles off-shore, setting up eddies and a tide-rip in certain weather conditions but in normal times giving no hint of any shallowing of the water. From the cliff top, near the ruinous remains of the sham fortress built by Lord Holland at the north end of Kingsgate Bay, coasters and small craft can be seen cutting the corner on their way into the Thames. Since the war several vessels have gone aground here, among them a grain elevator on its way from the Thames to a Russian port which broke its tow in an easterly gale. It was driven ashore right up against the cliffs but no lives were lost thanks to the efforts of the Coastguard with a breeches-buoy and the Margate lifeboat.

After the loss of the *Northern Belle* in 1857, described in detail later, the R.N.L.I. decided to establish a station here in 1862. The lifeboats already at Margate and Broadstairs were heavy, beamy boats designed to operate off-shore, but a vessel cutting the corner and going aground close in would be in a position where the scour of the tide and the shallow rock-strewn waters would make it difficult for the larger boats to be used successfully. Hence a small light draught boat would be essential, especially one which could be launched under the lee of the wreck.

There was already a gap-way through the cliffs used by fishermen, and by farmers collecting seaweed to manure their fields. This was widened sufficiently to take a two-wheeled launching trolley and the former Dungeness boat *Brave Robert Shedden* and her carriage were renovated for the purpose. She had the distinction of being the smallest lifeboat in the R.N.L.I. fleet, being a narrow single-banked boat rowing six oars and built by Forrestt of Limehouse. A local committee was formed to manage the station, the crew was drawn from the Coastguard Station in the bay and money was raised locally for a boat-house to be built at the head of the gap. At high water the boat could launch off a hard beach and efforts were made to flatten the chalk ridges to enable her to be hauled out and launched successfully at low water. The weed-covered chalk plateau on the shore still shows traces of this levelling work but of the boat-house only the cement foundation remains.

Standing at the bottom of the gap in an on-shore gale, with the waves battering at the chalk archway, one can visualise today the difficulties of launching and the

Kingsgate lifeboat *Thomas Chapman* and her crew of Coastguards in front of the lifeboat house. Date uncertain.   *W. Honey*

constant trouble these early lifeboatmen had with the gap-way. Now it is fenced off and littered with fallen chalk boulders.

The lifeboat crew found the original carriage unhandy for use in the gap-way, the lifeboat herself was difficult to right when capsized in the surf. After standing by the emigrant ship *Amazon* of London she was replaced by a second, *Brave Robert Shedden*, also built by Forrestt. Still there was trouble with the gap, the use of horses to pull the lifeboat carriage presented many problems so a winch and chain were transferred from Dover in 1864. With this equipment the work proved less arduous and the *Brave Robert Shedden* was launched successfully in January, 1866 to the help of the Norwegian brigantine *Fremad* of Bergen, aground in a north-easterly gale almost directly below Kingsgate Castle. Her crew of seven were rescued.

The launching and handling difficulties still continued so an effort was made to face up the gap-way with concrete, to reduce the falls of chalk, and in 1869 skids were brought into use to replace the carriage. These measures were only partially successful and the crew were reported to find the boat too heavy both ashore and afloat.

A new 30 foot × 8 foot boat pulling six oars was built especially for them by Forrestt which the Railway Company kindly delivered without charge. She was named *Thomas Chapman* after the Deputy Chairman of the R.N.L.I. and the crew found her much easier to haul both in launching and recovery. This satisfaction did not last long as reports were soon sent in that she was "cranky". The R.N.L.I. District Inspector came down to test her in heavy seas and she promptly capsized before she was clear of the land, fortunately without casualties. As a result of this her beam was increased and the sail removed. It was in this boat that a further life-saving mission was undertaken on 23rd February, 1880, when the ketch, *Forager* of Portsmouth, went aground near Kingsgate Castle. Unable to get off and with the wind piping up from east-north-east and a heavy sea, the *Thomas Chapman* was launched to rescue the crew of four, and then helped to get her off and escorted her, under tow, to Ramsgate. A second *Thomas Chapman*, built by Woolfe of Shadwell, was here until 1889 when she was replaced by a pulling and sailing lifeboat with the same name. However, the number of calls decreased so considerably that, in 1897, it was decided to close the station.

It is always sad to visit a seaport or coastal town which has had a lifeboat in the past but is now no longer a station. Not that this means that the place has declined in importance, but the modern motor lifeboat with its vastly increased radius of action, in constant radio-telephone contact with the shore, has made it unnecessary to maintain so many stations. The saddest part is that the spirit of service and self-sacrifice in trying to save life at sea might be lost and the record of life-saving forgotten. But this is certainly not the case with any of our Kent and Sussex stations even when the boat was withdrawn many years ago, for in nearly all these places there are still active Branches. The officials and voluntary helpers of these play a part which, though less spectacular, is of immense importance. Although not going afloat themselves, the hours of work they put in collecting funds in their devotion and enthusiasm for the cause of saving live provide the sinews without which our

Russian grain elevator ashore right up against the cliffs at Kingsgate, September 1946. Formerly the Kingsgate lifeboat would launch through a gap to the left.   *Author's collection*

voluntary service could not play its part. It is the very voluntary nature of the whole of the R.N.L.I. that is its strength and its excellence.

Broadstairs is just such a place, the jetty busy with small boats, a thriving sailing club, but no longer a lifeboat station as it is covered by Ramsgate's new 44 foot Waveney type and an inshore lifeboat as well. Edward Heath and Sir Alec Rose are among the well-known amateur sailors who learned to handle a boat off Viking Bay. Charles Dickens, whose connection with Broadstairs is commemorated by plaques on many buildings, spent holiday months here between 1837 and 1859. He wrote of the jetty, "We have a pier — a queer old wooden pier without the slightest pretensions to architecture and very picturesque in consequence. Boats are hauled up on it, ropes are coiled all over it, lobster pots, masts, oars, sails, ballast and rickety capstans make a perfect labyrinth of it."*

This jetty down at the foot of Harbour Street is the oldest building in Broadstairs, apart from St Peter's Church, and was erected by George Culmer in the late fifteenth century to protect the fishing boats. From here fishermen sailed as far as the Dogger Bank, Iceland, and the Banks of Newfoundland, fishing for cod. Luggers frequently went out "foying", or victualling passing ships. The name of Culmer is also to be seen on the ancient portcullis arch designed to guard the town against privateers, and the same family started the shipyard which occupied the area now devoted to the Council Entertainments department and the Garden on the Sands. The boat builder John White had married Mary Culmer in 1721 thus acquiring an interest in the yard. Between 1766 and 1824 fourteen ships of between 130 to 350 tons were built, the Naval brig *Desperate* of 180 tons being the last. As the quality of their work became increasingly well known, Thomas White and his son John moved to Cowes in the Isle of Wight, founding the firm of J. Samuel White and Company and specialising in the development of ships' lifeboats particularly for the P & O† fleet. A patent for these boats was taken out in 1843 and they were soon ordered for Coastguard posts all round the coast as well as for ships of the Royal Navy. A feature of these boats was the double skin of planking with waterproof material in between, the whole a fine example of skilful craftsmanship — but they would not self-right. As John White declared, a lifeboat "has no reason to capsize at all and there is no reason why she should".

In July 1850 Thomas and John White presented one of their 29 foot 6 inches × 6 foot 6 inches lifeboats to their home town and she was first called out on 6th March, 1851 to a brig, the *Mary White* that had gone on to the Goodwins during a heavy northerly gale. After a desperate struggle Coxswain Solomon Holbourn, who later became harbour-master, and his crew managed to bring the lifeboat within reach of the casualty. They got a line across, Holbourn and George Castle boarded her to help with the rescue and seven men had been transferred to safety when the rope parted. The lifeboat was swept clear leaving Holbourn, Castle, the captain of the ship and two other men on board. As it was obvious that the lifeboat would not be able to work back alongside, Holbourn and Castle sprang overboard to swim for it but before the others could follow the hulk overturned and they were lost.

*Our English Watering Place, by Charles Dickens 1858.

†By this abbreviation the famous shipping line, Peninsular and Oriental Steam Navigation Company, was best known. They provided the principal passenger service from Britain to India which ended in 1969 after 127 years.

Because of the strange coincidence of names the lifeboat was duly named *Mary White* in honour of her first service. Such enthusiasm was aroused in the county that a special song was composed about the rescue and the R.N.L.I. awarded silver medals for gallantry to all eight members of the lifeboat's crew. Delighted with this success John White presented Broadstairs with a second boat, the 30 foot × 8 foot 4 inch *Culmer White*, built in 1853. It was these two boats that were involved in the famous service to the American ship *Northern Belle* in January 1857.

This 1,000 ton vessel, bound from New York to London with a general cargo, anchored off Kingsgate in the early morning, caught by a foul tide and a north-easterly gale. With the storm increasing the main and mizzen masts were cut away to make her ride more easily but in spite of this her anchors began to drag, and the seas were making a clean breach over her decks. When news of her plight reached Broadstairs it was obvious that the lifeboat could not be rowed or sailed round against the gale to reach her. A crowd of volunteers harnessed themselves to the *Mary White's* trolley to haul her the two miles over the North Foreland and across the fields to Kingsgate Bay.

Meanwhile two Margate luggers, the *Ocean* and the *Eclipse*, had put men aboard to help the crew, but a third lugger, the *Victory*, which was standing by was suddenly overwhelmed by a mighty sea and lost with all hands. In the midst of a biting snow squall the *Northern Belle's* anchor cables parted at about midnight and, when day dawned on 8th January, the watchers on the clifftop and shore could make out 23 men lashed to the rigging of the one remaining mast. The *Mary White* immediately launched into the surf and though flung back onto the shore time and

Rescuing the crew of the *Northern Belle*, 1857.   *Drawing from The Illustrated London News*

again her gallant crew at last managed to go alongside, rescuing seven of the survivors. By this time the *Culmer White* had also arrived on the scene and, manned by a fresh crew of volunteers, took off 14 of the remainder, but she had to make yet another trip before they could persuade the captain and pilot to leave the wreck. The benumbed and exhausted sailors were taken to the *Captain Digby Inn*, where the second mate, a man of English descent, is said to have declared that none but Englishmen would have put off to the rescue in such a sea. The name plate of the *Northern Belle* with a list of the lifeboat crews can be seen in the *Rose Inn* in Albion Street.

With traffic in the channel increasing and these private lifeboats becoming less seaworthy, the R.N.L.I. was asked to take over the station in 1868. A new 36 foot × 9 foot 3 inch self-righter, built by Forrestt, was sent here, the gift of a Mrs Collins in memory of her son who had been lost at sea. This boat, the *Samuel Morrison Collins*, was on station here for twenty years, the harbour authorities allowing her to be kept on the pier and launched down a slipway which was constructed for £90. Nineteen years later a new slipway was built for £1,350. The increased cost was perhaps due to inflation and probably to the destruction of the woodwork of the older one by what was officially described as a "marine insect". In connection with this launching problem it is interesting to note that a private lifeboat was stationed here in 1880, presented by Edmund F. Davis of Sowell Street "to meet the need of a lighter boat that could be launched at any state of the tide". How long this boat was here is uncertain but the new slipway of 1887 would presumably have obviated the need for her.

From the balcony of the old boat-house on the jetty the surf beating over the Goodwins can be seen clearly, even on a moderately calm day. It was around the northern end of these treacherous sands that the Broadstairs lifeboats carried out most of their services, except when towed round to Margate as in the great storm of 1877, when they saved five people from the *Jane Cameron* as well as two ships, the *Mermaid* and the *Gleaner*.

The *Samuel Morrison Collins* had not been long on station when in October of 1869 she was called out to the help of the *Frank Shaw* of North Shields. This ship had anchored off the North Foreland in a northerly gale but, as the seas were sweeping her decks and she was in danger of sinking, her master slipped his anchor and drove before the wind in the hope of finding shelter under the lee of the land off Dover. But at 2 a.m. on the 19th she struck on the North Sand Head of the Goodwins.

Within 15 minutes she had broken in two, the masts and rigging carrying away to leeward, the crew crowding aft burnt distress flares which were sighted at Broadstairs and Ramsgate. At once Captain Elyard, the Honorary Secretary at Broadstairs, gathered a crew and the *Samuel Morrison Collins* set out running before the gale under reefed lugsails amid a confused sea. Arriving near the wreck they found the breakers pounding so savagely over the sands that they were unable to get alongside. The Ramsgate boat *Bradford* under Coxswain Jarman had arrived

Christopher Waud Bradford in Broadstairs Viking Bay.   *Author's collection*

at the scene towed by the steam tug *Aid* but was equally unsuccessful. While endeavouring to work in close enough to get a line aboard both lifeboats went aground on the falling tide and had to remain there with the surf driving into them some 200 yards to leeward of the wreck. The ebb was very strong, the seas so heavy that when the shipwrecked crew tried to launch their gig it was instantly dashed to pieces. They managed to get another boat away and six of them, landing on the sands, contrived to wade to the *Samuel Morrison Collins.* The rest followed, helped by a life-line, but in spite of this six were swept away and drowned. Of the survivors 13 reached the Broadstairs boat and one was picked up by Ramsgate.

There the two lifeboats had to remain, pounding in the surf, till the tide made sufficiently for them to drive off to the *Aid* which towed both boats to Ramsgate Harbour. It was 10 p.m. when they reached safety at last, being welcomed by wildly cheering crowds. For his part in the rescue Captain Elyard was awarded the silver medal; and in 1896 he was further honoured with the gold medal, having been concerned in the rescue of 49 lives.

Among the 84 service launches of the *Samuel Morrison Collins* another particularly notable one was in March 1871 to the barque *Iden* of Bergen, in conjunction with the *Bradford* of Ramsgate. As the master, Captain Meidall, wrote, "The noble boats under the able and skilful management of their persevering crews came out from the land at daybreak and dashed fearlessly into the foaming breakers, crossed the boiling sand, and at very great risk (the sea breaking heavily into them as they approached) succeeded in reaching the ship and lying alongside to our rescue." As the two lifeboats left the wreck they had to drive across the sands to leeward, for three hours being swept by the surf, till at last they reached the tug which towed them into Ramsgate at about 3 p.m. No wonder that Charles Dickens wrote in *Our English Watering Place*, "Let a gale arise and swell into a storm, let a sea run that might appal the stoutest heart that ever beat, let the

35

light-boat on those dangerous sands throw a rocket up into the night, or let them hear through the angry roar the signal guns of a ship in distress, these men spring up into activity so dauntless, so valiant and heroic, that the world cannot surpass it."

Dauntless the lifeboatmen certainly were, and they had need to be for nearly all the services on the Goodwins were tough and dangerous. Perhaps the service to the brig *Defender* of Sunderland in 1878 brought the Broadstairs crew nearest to disaster when the lifeboat, running in towards the wreck, was struck broadside on by a tremendous sea which threw her on her beam ends, filled her with water and washed her helplessly away to leeward. Brought to by her anchor she was preparing to face the smother again when the *Bradford* arrived towed by the *Aid* and veered down to rescue the shipwrecked crew. The same skill and fearless endeavour was shown by the men of the Broadstairs lugger *Florence Nightingale* when they saved 23 men from the steamer *Glendale* of Newcastle on the Goodwins the following year.

Finally having saved around a hundred lives the *Samuel Morrison Collins* was withdrawn, her place being taken by the *Christopher Waud Bradford*, ON 189, a 39 foot 2 inch × 8 foot 11 inch self-righter, built by Woolfe. Her donor, Mr George Motley Waud, had originally intended her for service on the Goodwin Sands from Ramsgate, but as another new boat was already earmarked for that station she came instead to Broadstairs.

William Foreman, who had been coxswain of the *Samuel Morrison Collins* for thirteen years, took over the new boat and was at the helm for many of her 52 services and was awarded the silver medal. He was succeeded by Jethro Miller Pettit, also awarded the silver medal in 1901. Both these were members of old Broadstairs sea-faring families and they carried on the tradition of skill and bravery which led to the Australian licensee of the *Prince Albert Inn* publishing a poem in 1895 in honour of Broadstairs lifeboatmen, the proceeds from the sale of it at ½d a copy to go to the local Philanthropic Association. Frequently the jetty also saw the arrival of shipwrecked crews aboard the North Deal or Walmer lifeboats, for after a service on the Goodwins in a southerly gale Broadstairs would be the most convenient landing-place to leeward.

In 1896 ON 189 was found to be defective so she was withdrawn and broken up, her place being taken by the self-righter *Francis Forbes Barton*, 40 foot × 10 foot 4 inch, ON 399, built by Rutherford of Birkenhead. She was on duty from 1897 to 1912 when the station was closed. Afterwards she did duty as a reserve lifeboat and served at the North Deal War Emergency Station from 1915 to 1921 and at North Deal in 1924. James Foreman became her coxswain, "Shah" Hiller was second coxswain, the bowman was S. J. Pettit, and among the crew were Crooms and Waleses.

In this boat the gallant story continued. On 115 services 77 lives were rescued, most of them again from the area of the Goodwins and it was during this time that the only casualties were suffered, Bowman Pettit dying from exposure and T. Wales collapsing with a heart attack after helping to haul the boat back up the slipway using the old capstan which still stands on the head of Broadstairs jetty. In 1905 in a north-westerly gale she was out all night searching for the schooner *Volunteer* of Caernarvon, but on the morning of 19th January the wreck was at last sighted and the numbed and exhausted crew of four who had spent 8 hours in the rigging beaten by spray were brought safely ashore.

A final appreciation of Broadstairs Lifeboat Station whose 275 launches resulted in the rescue of 269 lives and the winning of one gold and eleven silver medals, is provided by the late Miss O. M. Raven in her book *I Remember Perfectly Well*. "On stormy winter nights," she writes, "we were sometimes awakened by the boom of a gun, then silence, broken by the sound of the heavy running steps of our fishermen off to man the lifeboat. Peering through the curtains we could see the flickering of lanterns, and above the wind could hear the shouts of men, the creak, creak of the boat as she was shaken loose from her hold on the slipway, and the low roar as she slipped down to plunge deep in the water and rise again gallantly to her search for a distressed vessel. By morning she would be back and ready to be hauled up the slipway, and the wooden spokes of the capstan manned by sailors and bigger boys clattered and clicked as the tow-rope wound round his large girth. What heroes and friends they were, those jolly Pettits, Crooms and Hillers."

The companion station of Ramsgate which now covers the Broadstairs area has one of the longest histories of life-saving in the country, particularly so because of its position opposite the North Sand Head of the Goodwins. It is appropriate here to give more detail of these sands with which the history of lifeboat work in this section of the coast is so tightly woven.

The Goodwins are a great expanse of sand, partly uncovered at low water and having only a fathom or two over them at high tide, stretching for some ten and a half miles in length by four and a half breadth at their widest part. In shape they resemble a hand pointing south with the thumb projecting towards the Kentish shore and are intersected by innumerable channels known only to the local

The last Broadstairs lifeboat, *Francis Forbes Barton* on the jetty slipway (c. 1904). Coxswain at the time of this picture was James Foreman, "Shah" Hiller was Second Coxswain, Bill ("Nelson"), Jimmy, Teddy and Albert Croom were among the crew, as was Jack Hiller. She was later the North Deal reserve lifeboat 1915-1921.

From an old postcard

Coxswain Charles Fish of Ramsgate 1870-1891.

R.N.L.I.

fishermen. Even on a calm day waves fret against this desolate bank of firm hard sand where it is uncovered, and the sand is soft and sinking beneath the water. When storm winds rage the breaking seas clap together dashing their foam twenty and thirty feet into the air. For more than two centuries inventors have wrestled with the problem of warning ships of the perils of this grim place and at one time it was even suggested that a harbour of refuge might be built on part of the sands. Borings were made by Trinity House and other bodies in a search for a firm base on which to erect a warning beacon but their findings varied. The Trinity House survey of 1817 recorded blue clay at 15 feet with chalk beneath whereas Admiral Bullock in 1840 found the sand so dense that his boring tool broke at seven and a half feet. The much more thorough survey by Sir J. H. Pelly in 1849 revealed sand to 46 feet followed by shells, small stones, decayed wood and yet more sand before a stable base was reached at 78 feet. Under these circumstances Trinity House decided to stick to light vessels, the North Goodwin being the first in 1795, the Gull in 1809, South Sand Head in 1855 and the East Goodwin in 1874. The Gull was sunk in collision in 1929 and her replacement was renamed the Brake; but after the war this was no longer found necessary, the three main lightships and fifteen buoys being considered sufficient.

In an easterly gale the Sands provide a natural bulwark against the storm and in the eighteenth and nineteenth centuries hundreds of ships found shelter between them and the Deal shore, in the anchorage known as the Downs. But if the wind swung northerly or southerly they would have to up-anchor and run for it to avoid disaster.

The Royal Harbour of Ramsgate, built at first as a harbour of refuge, has a long history of seafaring, the luggers from this place ranging the Sands, carrying victuals to stormbound vessels, providing pilotage and engaging in salvage operations with outstanding daring. George IV sailed from here to his dominions in Hanover, there was an important fleet of fishing smacks, a fish market, and, with the growth of seaside holidays and the coming of the railway, a great increase in pleasure boating, the Royal Temple Yacht Club being founded in 1857. To this port, also, came the pleasure steamers from London, beating their way past the Foreland, the powerful *Eagle* and *Royal Sovereign*, the tug pleasure steamer *Conqueror*, the smaller *Myleta* and *Edward William* which plied between here and Folkestone. These latter boats were very under-powered and there is a story that the captain of *Myleta* with paddles thrashing unavailingly against a difficult tide saw his wife aboard a tram speeding across the cornfields behind Dumpton Gap and easily outdistancing his vessel.

It seems only natural that Lionel Lukin should entrust his *Experiment* to a Ramsgate man for testing and that the Harbour Trustees should realise the need for a lifeboat as early as 1802, twenty-two years before the founding of the R.N.L.I. Henry Greathead of South Shields, who had earlier built the *Original* for service at the mouth of the Tyne, supplied their first boat. Unfortunately no details survive either of her or the service she gave. It is thought she was probably 31 foot × 10½ foot, clinker built, with both bow and stern pointed and rising sharply, with a

Ramsgate harbour tug *Vulcan* towing the *Bradford* out to the *Indian Chief*, 5th January, 1881. Oil-colour by Broome originally in the possession of an old Margate lifeboatman.

P. H. Williamson

steering-oar and packings of cork at bow, stern and round the gunwales to provide additional buoyancy. The station lapsed in about 1824 but was re-opened again in 1852 when the Harbour Trustees purchased a lifeboat built by James Beeching of Great Yarmouth. He had won the prize offered by the Duke of Northumberland in 1851 for the best model of a lifeboat, and the boat purchased followed that design being 36 foot × 9½ foot pulling 12 oars, rigged with lug foresail and mizzen, and steered by rudder. Raised air-cases fore and aft, 2¼ tons of water ballast and an iron keel made her self-right. This boat was still in service when the R.N.L.I. took over the station in 1865 and had proved herself to be an admirable boat. For the first ten years James Hogben was coxswain and by 1857 he had taken part in so many gallant rescues that the R.N.L.I. awarded him the silver medal. In 1858 the lifeboat journal recorded that the *Northumberland* lifeboat had been off the Goodwins no less than 60 or 70 times in the past five years. Services to the French schooner *Eleanore* when only the captain was saved, to a Dutch schooner, to the *Violet* mail steamer are but a few at the start of a tremendous record.

Family links with the lifeboat were quickly forged. Throughout the long history of the station the names of various well-known fishing or lugger-owning families recur — as in so many of our lifeboat communities. There have been five generations of Coopers in "the boat", for example, Tommy Cooper succeeding Arthur Verrion as coxswain from 1963 to 1975 with forty-five years in the boat, and his son now being in the crew. The ancestor of Arthur Verrion who became coxswain in 1953, after being in the crew since 1920, was aboard the *Bradford* together with old and young Tom Cooper at the time of the famous *Indian Chief* rescue in 1881. Many members of the crew were fishermen, others like Stephen Penney, who served in the boat for fifty-five years, linked fishing with pleasure-boat owning, his *Avona* won the sailing race at the regatta for twenty-six years in succession. He was master of the famous lugger *Champion*, was mentioned by Charles Dickens and hovelled cargoes and did general salvage work on the Goodwins. One of the ancestors of Douglas Kirkaldie, who was coxswain from 1946-58, owned a vessel that brought stone from Shoreham for the building of the harbour. Douglas Kirkaldie himself was harbour pilot and official boatman for the Missions to Seamen as well as being a salvage expert concerned in salving, among others, the *Helena Modjeska* and the *Fort Vermilion* from the Goodwins.

When the R.N.L.I. took over the station in 1865 a new 40 foot × 10 foot 4 inch boat of 19 oars was specially built for towing by Forrestt with money raised by the City of Bradford Lifeboat Fund and named the *Bradford*. While she was being built the tug *Aid* went down to Selsey to fetch the lifeboat *Friend* to do temporary duty and during 1865 she rescued twenty-three. During the eleven years the *Bradford* was on station no less than 344 lives were saved and many wrecked vessels were brought safely into harbour by the combined efforts of the lifeboatmen and the steam tugs *Aid* and *Vulcan*. Indeed nearly all the rescues were the direct result of joint efforts by tug and lifeboat, often in conjunction with lifeboats from Broadstairs, North Deal, Walmer and Kingsdown.

The third *Bradford* 42 foot × 11 foot built by Woolfe in 1895.   *R.N.L.I.*

Danger and tragedy marked nearly every service. In December 1870 the *Bradford* was towed by the *Aid* to the help of the ship *Providence* aground on the south-east Calliper in a north-easterly gale. She veered down on the wreck, getting a hawser on board, down which the captain and crew tried to slide into the lifeboat. The captain was washed off by heavy surf but was grabbed and hauled into the boat. Masts and spars came crashing as the ship broke up. Another crew member was swept off the lifeline and also rescued after a hard struggle but his mate was swept away and drowned. One terrified apprentice was left on board screaming for help. For half an hour the lifeboatmen tried to reach him but suddenly a huge wave shattered the ship and swept him away. He seemed quite dead when they reached him, but he was at length resuscitated and saved. The rest of the crew were picked up from the ship's boat by a passing vessel.

First under Isaac Jarman who was coxswain at the time of the *Frank Shaw* service, then under the famous Charles Fish, the *Bradford* continued her amazing series of rescues. The *Marie Antoinette* of Nantes went onto the North Sand Head in water so shallow that the lifeboat could not get nearer than 50 fathoms. Four of the lifeboatmen jumped into the water and waded to the vessel where they tried for three hours or more to persuade the crew to leave and wade to the lifeboat through the boiling surf with the aid of life-lines. At length all did so except for the captain, but before he could leave the schooner suddenly turned turtle. They imagined he

41

s.s. *Western Farmer* of New York, from the stern of which Coxswain Douglas Kirkaldie rescued the captain and three seamen, winning the silver medal.   *Photograph by Planet. R.N.L.I.*

must have perished but he had lashed himself to a spar and was picked up, more dead than alive, by a Broadstairs lugger hovering near the Sands.

The daring and courage of these lifeboatmen of old was matched by the bravery and fine seamanship of the men of the harbour tugs which would tow the lifeboat through the wildest weather to windward of the wreck. The lifeboat would then row, sail, or veer down on her anchor cable to effect the rescue. It is fitting that masters and men of the tugs should have been honoured by the R.N.L.I. Coxswain Jarman was awarded the silver medal in 1862 and a second clasp to it in 1871, David Reading of the harbour tug a silver medal in 1872, and similar awards were made to Mate J. Simpson and Engineer W. Wherrier four years later. Albert Page, tug master at the *Indian Chief* rescue was awarded the silver medal, a second clasp in 1892 and a third in 1898. In all the R.N.L.I. has awarded 2 gold and 37 silver medals to men of Ramsgate, figures which are the highest for any station in Kent.

The first gold medal award was to Coxswain Charles Fish for his skill and determination in rescuing 12 men from the barque *Indian Chief*, one of the greatest lifeboat services of all time. Silver medals were awarded to the 11 members of the lifeboat crew as well as to the master and crew of the tug *Vulcan*. On 5th January, 1881, at 2.30 a.m. the *Indian Chief* bound for Yokohama from Middlesborough piled up on the Long Sand in an easterly gale having missed stays. She was right out in the Thames Estuary some 30 miles from Ramsgate and news of her plight did not reach the harbour till noon, but at once the *Bradford*, the second of this name, put out in tow of the tug *Vulcan*. The first *Bradford* had been damaged in collision with the *Vulcan* four years earlier. It was dark by the time they reached the Kentish Knock lightship but in spite of being given bearings it was impossible to find her under such conditions. In heavy seas, in darkness and with a bitter gale blowing Coxswain Fish and his crew refused to give up the search. All through the long bitterly cold night, exposed to the whole fury of the gale, amid dangerous sands tug and lifeboat held position, the tug, under Albert Page, suffering damage to deckhouses and sponsons, the lifeboatmen huddling together for warmth and to gain some shelter from the biting cold and driving spray.

At daybreak they sighted the wreck. Only the foremast still stood, with 12 men lashed to the rigging. The captain and the other 16 crew had been drowned when the mainmast and mizzen went over-side. It was clear that these survivors must be rescued without delay, so the coxswain drove his boat right into the smother of broken water and, with the greatest difficulty, worked nearer to the wreck. The mate of the *Indian Chief* declared afterwards that he did not believe that even a lifeboat could face the surf, "for," he said, "the sea was frightful all to windward of the Sand and over it a tremendous play of broken waters, raging one with another, making the whole surface resemble a boiling cauldron. Yet they never swerved a hair's breadth. We could see the crew — twelve of them — sitting on the thwarts, all looking our way, motionless as carved figures and there was not a stir among them as, in an instant, the boat leapt from the crest of a towering sea right into the monstrous broken tumble. Over and over again the boat was buried but as regularly did she emerge with her crew fixedly looking our way and their oilskins and the light coloured side of the boat sparkling in the sunshine while the coxswain, leaning forward from the helm, watched our ship with a face of iron."

At last the *Bradford* succeeded in closing the wreck and all twelve survivors were rescued. It was 2 p.m. before tug and lifeboat reached Ramsgate having been out in that furious bitter gale for 26 hours. One of the survivors, the second mate, died in the lifeboat on the way back and was buried in the Sailors' Church by the harbour. His name was Howard Primrose Fraser. The wife of the mate of the *Vulcan* who was expecting a baby, named it after him; and this Howard Primrose Knight was coxswain of Ramsgate lifeboat at the time of Dunkirk, serving for more than forty-eight years in the boat.

This same lifeboat, the second *Bradford*, (44 foot × 11 foot 1 inch built by Woolfe) in the course of saving the amazing total of 405 lives, was involved in a curious incident when a Spanish steamer the *Santa Rosa*, laden with iron ore for Middlesborough, went on the Goodwins in November 1885. The weather was foggy but the local lugger *Champion* owned by Stephen Penney was continually plying to and fro, taking out men to jettison the cargo and ferrying food and stores. One evening, when she had been stuck fast for a record nine days, she drove off. At once the lifeboat and the *Vulcan* put out in response to flares and started to drag the ship at top speed towards the harbour, helped by another tug, the *Duoro*. So strained was the ship that water was pouring into her so fast that pumps and frenzied bailing could scarcely keep it in check. By the time they were within a few cable lengths of the harbour mouth the crew were all on deck, the water lapping over her sides. Just as they came through the harbour entrance she settled down, almost opposite the landing stage; and when she was later salvaged and put on the slipway, it was found that the bottom plates were broken and some actually hanging down as a result of the pounding she had received. The *Santa Rosa* still holds the record for the longest stay on the Goodwins and surviving although the *Fort Vermilion*, in 1946, ran her close. By a strange coincidence the latter vessel was also laden with iron ore for Middlesborough. Clark Russell's comments, written in 1889, seem particularly appropriate in view of the damage to the *Santa Rosa*. He refers to the sad decline in importance of Ramsgate harbour but then refers to the lifeboat work as its chief claim to fame. "There is always a steamer at hand night and day," he writes, "to tow the lifeboat out to where the stranded craft lies . . . where in the blackness of the thunderous midnight, she rests quivering to the Titan blows of the Goodwin breakers."

Charles Fish retired in 1891 after twenty-one years as coxswain, having assisted in the saving of the astonishing total of 877 lives and being awarded the second clasp to the gold medal on his retirement. His last few years of service were in the third *Bradford*, a 40 foot 2 inch × 10 foot self-righter with four water ballast tanks and sliding keel, ON 117, built by Forrestt which was on station till 1893.

Shortly before his retirement, in January 1891, exactly ten years after his service to the *Indian Chief*, he took this boat out into a blinding snow storm, towed by the new *Aid*, which had replaced the older tug of the same name, in answer to flares from the Gull lightship. North Deal lifeboat under Coxswain Roberts had also put out but in the bitter east-north-east gale had to tack to and fro to reach the position whereas the *Bradford*, under tow and with wind abaft the beam, could make much better headway. The vessel on the Goodwins was found to be a three-master, the *Crocodile* which had missed stays and gone onto the northern edge of the Sands. She lay there, with the seas pounding at her, broadside on. Coxswain Fish had Tom Cooper with him as second coxswain just as he did at the *Indian Chief* rescue; but this time there was no need to lay-to all night. They cast off the tow, ran in close, dropped anchor and began to veer down towards the wreck, the deck of which was now under water and the crew clinging to the rigging of the mizzen. As they came near the wreck a huge sea struck them, snapped their cable like pack-thread and sent the *Bradford* reeling across the shallows. She put on sail at once and they tacked clear to where the *Aid* was waiting to leeward. The tug again dragged them up to windward for another attempt, which was successful, for they veered alongside and the numbed sailors managed to swing themselves down the rigging and into the boat; all except the captain who fell to his death. Just as they completed the rescue the North Deal boat, *Mary Somerville*, arrived under storm canvas too late to help. An idea of the toughness and endurance of these men may be gained by the fact that within an hour of reaching harbour they were out again to pick up the crew of the collier, *Glance*, which had sunk after a collision with her sister ship, *Glide* whose crew had been rescued by Broadstairs.

In 1893 yet another *Bradford* came on station, 42 foot × 11 foot, pulling 12 oars, ON 350 and built by Woolfe. Although launched on a large number of occasions, 221 times, she was actually involved in less saving of life. In view of the South Goodwin disaster of 1954 when Ramsgate lifeboat stood by for 13 hours, it is interesting that one of her services was, in September 1903, to the South Goodwin lightship of those days — which had gone adrift. This was in a whole gale from the north-north-west, the seas so heavy that it was doubtful if the tug would be able to tow the lifeboat to the given position. They managed to struggle to within two miles but turned back as the more powerful Dover tug was seen to be at hand and taking the lightship in tow.

It was in the next lifeboat, the *Charles and Susanna Stephens*, a 42 foot × 12 foot self-righter, ON 537, built by Thames Ironworks, that Coxswain Cooper won a silver medal from the King of Denmark for his rescue of the crew of seven from the schooner *Danmark* in 1911. Five years later, on 20th November, 1916, he carried out a further service of the utmost danger and difficulty to the s.s. *Sibiria* of New York which was wrecked on the Goodwins during a gale spoken of as the worst for many years. On the 19th, North Deal's *Charles Dibdin* rescued the crew of the *Val Salice* in conditions of appalling difficulty, but some four hours afterwards distress signals were seen from a large steamer aground in the same area. By this time the wind had reached hurricane force, the Deal reserve boat was unable to reach the wreck so Ramsgate tried. While endeavouring to veer down after being constantly filled with water and almost capsized, the cable parted, a bollard being torn clean

Wreck of South Goodwin lightship, 28th November, 1954. *R.N.L.I.*

out and several of the crew injured. Coxswain Cooper returned to harbour for repairs and additional crew and then set out again, but by the time he reached the Sands, Kingsdown's *Charles Hargrave* had managed to save the 52 shipwrecked sailors. For this service he was awarded the silver medal by the R.N.L.I. and in a further service to the *Piave* of New Jersey in 1919, when 23 of the crew were rescued, he was awarded a gold watch by the President of the United States.

All these services were performed by the old pulling and sailing lifeboats when brawn and muscle coupled with superb seamanship were the essentials; but by this time the internal combustion engine was providing a valid alternative — at first only as an auxiliary but later as the main propulsion. In 1906 the fourth *Bradford* was taken from reserve and fitted with a 30 h.p. Tylor engine and then underwent extensive trials. As a result when *Charles and Susanna Stephens* was withdrawn, after 165 service launches and with 294 lives saved, in 1925, her replacement was a motor lifeboat. She was the *Prudential*, a 48 foot × 13 foot motor boat, ON 697, of the special Ramsgate class and built by S. E. Saunders of Cowes. This splendid boat was on station for twenty-seven arduous years between 1926 and 1953 during which the number of lives rescued was 330; this total excludes the outstanding war-time service when she went across to Dunkirk, saving 2,800 men. Throughout the war years she was busy, her coxswain and crew defying the additional perils of aerial bombardment and mines to save 170 lives.

Not long after the war, in May 1947, the *Newhall Hills*, a 10,000 ton tanker, was in collision off the Goodwins with the Swedish motor vessel *Monica*. There was an explosion in number one and two holds of the tanker and she caught fire as the *Prudential* made for the scene. She stood by ready to give help but shortly after 1.40 p.m. the bow broke away and sank. Lifeboatmen assisted in getting tow-lines from

Arthur Verrion of Ramsgate, Coxswain 1953-1963.
Photograph by East Kent Times.   R.N.L.I.

Michael and Lily Davis, Watson type lifeboat entering Ramsgate harbour.   *R.N.L.I.*

tugs secured on board, then escorted the tanker to Sheerness, having been away on service for 32 hours. A quick glance through Coxswain Kirkaldie's log book shows an astonishing variety of services of which this is only one instance. Yachts towed into harbour, chasing and recovering a local trawler whose crew had been overcome by fumes in the engine-room, piloting ships clear of the Goodwins after they had been aground, searches for "ditched" aircraft, assisting a motor-boat which had stuck on its own anchor-fluke — all these and more are succinctly entered. In one week in 1951 the lifeboat was on service three times, twice on successive days. What gives an even better idea of the importance of the station is that, when he retired in 1952, Douglas Kirkaldie had been in charge on 140 services since his appointment in 1946. His most dangerous mission, however, was to the s.s. *Western Farmer* of New York, in collision with a Norwegian tanker 18 miles east-south-east of Ramsgate. In a very heavy sea the *Prudential* reached the position at 8.45 p.m. on 20th August, 1952 to find the *Western Farmer* extensively damaged. Tugs soon arrived but the ship began to break up, the *Prudential* taking aboard seven members of the crew. Soon after the order to abandon ship, the fore part of the vessel broke away and capsized. With increasing difficulty, as every wave breaking aboard smothered the decks with escaped fuel oil, the *Prudential* took aboard the men from one of the ship's boats and picked up one survivor from the water. The Dover lifeboat, also now on the scene, picked up 13 from the second ship's boat. Suddenly, in the glare of his searchlight, the coxswain thought he detected a shadow move on the stern portion of the ship which was partly awash and drifting. Without hesitation, although it was clear that it might heel over and capsize at any moment, he took the *Prudential* alongside and succeeded in taking off the captain and three others who had been left on the stern. The *Prudential*, covered in fuel oil, did not get back to Ramsgate till 3.15 a.m. and for this service Coxswain Kirkaldie was awarded the silver medal.

Since then the *Michael and Lily Davis*, a 46 foot 9 inch × 12 foot 9 inch Watson, ON 901, built by J. Samuel White did duty here until 1976, in this period saving 309 lives under Coxswains Arthur Verrion, Tommy Cooper and Herbert Goldfinch. It was during this time that the total number of lives rescued by Ramsgate lifeboats exceeded 2,000 as recorded by the R.N.L.I.

It was in the *Michael and Lily Davis* that Arthur Verrion carried out a most arduous and tragic service in 1954. During a terrible storm, with winds gusting up to 60 m.p.h., the South Goodwin lightship went adrift and at about 3.20 a.m. the lifeboat put out. She stood by the last reported position of the lightship and at dawn saw the wreck hard and fast aground with the surf breaking over her. A U.S.A.F. amphibian from Manston circled the place and reported seeing no sign of life, but a U.S. helicopter which joined in the action lowered a noose and the lifeboatmen saw, to their amazement, a man hoisted up into the plane. Because of the way the wreck was canted over on its side away from them they had not spotted him from their position a few hundred yards distant. The rescued man was a bird watcher who had been observing bird migration for the Ministry of Agriculture, and he was the sole survivor. The lifeboatmen returned to harbour, caked with salt and numb with cold, but after a change of clothing and some food they returned to the scene until the search for survivors was called off that evening. They had been out on service in appalling conditions for 14 hours.

A service with a happier outcome was in October 1968 when the *Michael and Lily Davis* put out to the 17 ton yacht *Lungta* aground on the bar outside the harbour. Coxswain Cooper anchored in one and a half fathoms to windward of her and veered down, firing a rocket line and connecting a tow. However this was insufficiently made fast aboard the yacht; as soon as the lifeboat began the tow the line slipped and the *Lungta* was swept into an even more precarious position. Again the lifeboat went to windward and veered down, at times hitting the bottom, till at last a secure tow was effected and the yacht and her four occupants brought to safety after a service lasting three hours. This was the most recent service to receive a special award, Coxswain Cooper receiving the thanks of the Institution on vellum. Herbert Goldfinch, who succeeded him, after being second coxswain for a number of years, also had difficult situations to face, among others, on service to the German yacht *Albas* which went on to the north end of the Goodwins in a heavy south-west gale. The lifeboat could not approach nearer than half a mile because of the shoal water, but two of the crew, T. Hurst and M. Petts, waded through the surf to lead the four shipwrecked crew to the lifeboat. Later when the tide re-floated the vessel men were put aboard and she was towed to Ramsgate but had to be beached just outside the harbour as she was about to sink.

Now the new 44 foot Waveney class *Ralph and Joy Swann,* built by the Bideford shipyard, and named in 1976 by H.R.H. The Duchess of Kent, is on station under R. Cannon whose father was for seventeen and a half years mechanic of the previous boat. With her superior speed of 16 knots this fine boat and her dedicated crew will undoubtedly maintain the high traditions of this important station, assisted by the I.L.B. serving here since 1969.

This diagram of the Goodwin Sands was drawn by former lifeboat coxswain Douglas Kirkaldie. Since then the lightships and several buoys have been moved. The figure 3 in a circle indicates where the South Goodwin lightship was and X where she lay as shown in the picture on page 45.

By courtesy of the East Kent Times

49

CHAPTER THREE

THE GOODWIN SANDS

North Deal, Walmer and Kingsdown

IMMEDIATELY opposite the Goodwins lies the stony beach of Deal with the fishing boats drawn up on the strand opposite their windlasses and the fretting waves constantly altering the contours of the shingle. At the Walmer end of the beach stands the lifeboat on her launching turn-table just seaward of the lifeboat house, a curiously chapel-like building, the bell above it adding to this impression. This bell is still used to call out the crew. The shingle beach drops away sharply and greasy wooden baulks or skids have to be dragged into place to give her a clear run into the sea from her launching ways. Even on a calm day the rush down the shingle on these skids is an extraordinary experience, the boat canted over on her bilge keel bumping and thundering her way into the foremost breakers, a haul-off warp ready in case her momentum is insufficient to carry her safely clear of the first few waves.

For many centuries launching, in this area, has been effected in much the same fashion and there has always been a busy sea-faring community. In earliest times the threat of invasion contributed much to its importance. Just as Julius Caesar drove his galleys ashore at Walmer because it was the first place along the coast that the high chalk cliffs gave way to a beach and an easy access inland, so the constant threat from across the channel brought the Cinque Ports fleet to anchor in the Downs and Hubert de Burgh defeated the French here in 1215. Many historical figures landed on this part of the coast when crossing from France, among them Thomas à Becket when returning from exile and just before he was slain in Canterbury Cathedral. Henry VIII gathered 400 ships in the Downs for the invasion of France and fearing retaliation fortified the place with strong castles shaped like the Tudor Rose. From this period dates the office of Lord Warden of the Cinque Ports whose official residence is Walmer Castle and the establishment of a naval yard which continued in operation till 1863. There was a constant coming and going of ships, and the inhabitants of Deal, Walmer and Kingsdown were constantly involved in supplying provisions, providing pilotage, and salving ships and cargoes in danger off their shores. One writer, G. B. Gattie, has mentioned that in 1836 as many as 400 ships were lying in the Downs to ride out a storm of which some 250 drove away, foundered, were dismasted or went on to the Goodwins.

The earliest mention of a rescue is in 1563 when the Earl of Warwick, who had just been appointed Governor of Newhaven by Elizabeth I, was swept in his ship northward as far as the Small Downs. As his boat the *New Barke* was in danger he and his staff were taken ashore by a boat from Deal. Over the centuries the Downs were the scene of battles, in particular between Blake and Van Tromp* as well as a base anchorage for the British Fleet. In the great storm of 1703, 13 men-of-war were

*The First Anglo-Dutch War (1652-4).

The great storm of 1703 when Admiral Sir Basil Beaumont and 13 men-of-war were wrecked on the Goodwins.   *W. Honey*

wrecked on the Goodwins, Admiral Sir Basil Beaumont and some 1,300 men being lost despite gallant efforts by the Mayor and various Deal boatmen who put off to the rescue and succeeded in saving 270. Here too Lord Nelson, as captain of the 28 gun *Albemarle*, had himself ferried out to his ship in a gale to make sure she was not endangered by other drifting vessels. "Even the Deal boatmen thought it impossible to get on board such was the violence of the storm. At length some of the most intrepid offered to make the attempt for 15 guineas, and to the astonishment and fear of all the beholders he embarked during the height of the tempest. With great difficulty and imminent danger he reached her."*

In 1805 the sorely damaged *Victory* lay here for three days with Lord Nelson's body on board, while all flags ashore flew at half mast and a nation mourned.

A more joyful spectacle is mentioned by G. B. Gattie† in 1842 when the entire fleet of 50 first class luggers from Deal, Walmer and Kingsdown, launched from the beach and sailed past Walmer Castle. Queen Victoria, Prince Albert and the Duke of Wellington who watched them from this vantage point were impressed by the skill of the hovellers in handling their vessels.

What types of craft did these dexterous seamen use? In the early years of the nineteenth century, when it is estimated there were about 1,000 men employed in

Life of Nelson by R. Southey, Everyman, Dent 1906.
†*Memorials of the Goodwin Sands,* 1890.

off-shore work, luggers were the principal boats used. These were very fine sea-boats, 40 foot × 13 foot, clinker built of elm, rigged with lugsails on fore and mizzen masts and carried a crew of over 20 men. Smaller counterparts, known locally as "cats", were equally fine sea-boats and were similarly rigged. Before Customs and Excise Officers reached their peak of efficiency in 1840 there was also a fair number of slim fast 40 footers along the beach and here—as on the shores of Romney Marsh—smugglers made many a successful "landing". Smaller craft still, but very typical, were the galley punts of 21 foot to 30 foot with a 7 foot beam. They carried a lugsail on a single mast stepped more or less amidships, had a crew of three or four and voyaged far westward down the channel to meet and offer to pilot incoming ships. The very perilous business of "hooking" a ship, referred to by the Reverend T. S. Treanor, in his *Heroes of the Goodwin Sands,* and being then towed by the vessel until she wished to drop her pilot was carried on exclusively by these galley punts. One curious feature of the early nineteenth century sailors of Deal was the wearing of tall hats and pumps.

All these craft were launched from the beach and all had a fairly identical rig so when the R.N.L.I. decided to establish lifeboat stations here, boats of similar general design and rig were used.

It is extremely difficult to differentiate between the various stations as they were all principally concerned with services to vessels on the Goodwins, frequently working in conjunction with one another. The record of their combined achievements is outstanding.

Walmer was the first established, in 1856, when a 30 foot × 7 foot 6 inch self-righter pulling 10 oars and built by Forrestt came on station. This was the

The first North Deal lifeboat, *Van Kook.*   R.N.L.I.

Royal Thames Yacht Club, being shortly followed in 1861 by a longer and heavier boat also given by the same Yacht Club and measuring 37 foot × 8 foot 4 inch. Despite their rescue of 21 lives between them it was soon obvious that an additional station should be established further northward as in many conditions of wind and tide the Walmer boat would be unable to "fetch" the casualty. To meet this problem the North Deal Station was established in 1865 and the self-righter the *Van Kook* of 40 foot × 10 foot and built by Forrestt was brought here. This boat was the gift of the artist E. W. Cooke who had exhibited a picture of the Ramsgate lifeboat in the Royal Academy.

The *Royal Thames Yacht Club* and *Van Kook* were involved in the service to the full-rigged ship *Iron Crown* in 1865 which in a south-south-west gale was driving and bumping over the Goodwin Sands. One of the Deal luggers *England's Glory* was also on the scene, and running in as close as she dared, six of her men were able to scramble aboard the casualty. The *Royal Thames Yacht Club* now dashed into the surf, but just as she luffed up alongside, a breaking sea sent her reeling away to leeward. The *Van Kook* under the experienced hands of Coxswains Wilds and Roberts managed to veer down on her anchor cable and put a further six men aboard. These skilful Deal boatmen knowing the sands and the run of the tide contrived to hurl a kedge anchor from high up on the fore yard and when the drift of the ship was checked other anchors were let go. As she lifted on the rising tide cables were made fast to tugs which were standing by and the *Iron Crown* was towed successfully into deep water in the Downs.

The following year it was decided to station yet another lifeboat at the near-by fishing village of Kingsdown and the 33 foot × 8 foot *Sabrina*, also built by Forrestt, was sent here. Thus the formidable Goodwins were now guarded by three lifeboats, all of them capable of facing the tremendous seas that stream over the Sands and which could quickly fill and sink the stoutest and heaviest of the luggers.

During the winter of 1866 in a bitter east-south-east gale, a number of ships in the Downs were in difficulties. Some of the larger luggers were at work supplying fresh anchors or pilots but with the gale increasing they had to make for shore. Soon vessels began to drag and drive onto the beach, among them the *Glendura* of Liverpool whose captain, realising the imminent danger, ran his ship straight onto the strand, as luck would have it directly opposite the Kingsdown Lifeboat House. As she struck he streamed a cork fender on the end of a line hoping that someone ashore might seize it and manage to rescue them. Coxswain Arnold and the Kingsdown crew, already assembled, saw the fender and, with the aid of the rope and their own haul-off warp, managed to claw the lifeboat through the 200 yards of breakers to the wreck. Over and over again the lifeboat was filled, the crew were drenched and numb with cold, but they struggled on. Five trips in all Coxswain Arnold had to make, with fresh crews each time, before all 29 survivors were brought ashore including the captain of *Glendura*, his wife and young son. After this service Jarvist Arnold found that his oilskin was so caked with ice that, when he managed to drag it off, it stood up on its own accord.

Richard (Dick Foss) Roberts (b. 1838 d. 1933). Second Coxswain 1865-1885, Coxswain 1885-1907.   *R.N.L.I.*

Jarvist Arnold, Coxswain of Kingsdown lifeboat 1866-1886.   *W. Honey*

For twenty years this tough and experienced old seaman was coxswain at Kingsdown as well as carrying on his profession as a Channel pilot. Throughout this period he was ably assisted by James Laming who succeeded him as coxswain in 1886. On one rescue mission they brought ashore 16 men from the barque *India* and were out for 12 hours in appalling conditions, the seas running mountains high. They crossed and re-crossed the Goodwins no less than four times, a feat that pays the greatest possible tribute to the skill of the coxswain and the staunch build of the *Sabrina*. It was in the second boat of this name, a slightly larger boat of 36 foot × 9 foot that Jarvist Arnold carried out his most famous rescue.

At 2.30 a.m. on the 17th December, 1872 the sound of signal guns and the burst of rockets mingled with the howl of a south-westerly gale to indicate a ship in distress on the Goodwins. The *Sabrina* and the Walmer boat, *Centurion*, a 36 foot × 9 foot 4 inch boat which had replaced the *Royal Thames Yacht Club* were launched to search for the wreck. Crossing the surf on the Goodwins and making for the southern end they found the large steamship *Sorrento* hard and fast aground. By the time they reached her the tide had fallen and both lifeboats were able to go alongside in the flying scud putting aboard a number of lifeboatmen to assist in lightening the ship, in the hope of getting her off on the next tide. The *Centurion* under Coxswain William Bushell lay alongside while *Sabrina* worked off into deeper water to lay out a kedge anchor to prevent the *Sorrento* from driving further onto the Sands. All hands aboard the steamer worked feverishly to clear the ship of water and jettison the cargo, but as morning came they realised she was doomed. Her back was broken and the sea poured in so swiftly that the pumps could not keep pace with it. Worse still, as the tide rose the gale increased and soon great waves were breaking on the steamer's quarter sweeping the decks and driving crew and lifeboatmen to the shelter of the bridge. As they waited their chance to abandon ship and leap into the Walmer lifeboat, a huge breaker drove down upon them tearing away the ship's boats, breaking the mooring cable which held the Walmer boat alongside and sending her spinning madly away amongst the wreckage. She was swept to leeward a full half-mile before she could be brought up by her anchor and, with only half her crew and wind and tide against her, could not regain the wreck. Seeing this Coxswain Arnold in *Sabrina* realised that his boat alone would have to effect the rescue, not only of the shipwrecked crew but also of the 14 lifeboatmen who had been helping on board the vessel. Forty-six lives were at stake, three of them his sons who had gone aboard the *Sorrento*. Carefully he veered down on his anchor cable, bent on a second cable so that *Sabrina* was riding to a full 160 fathoms* but the tide kept sweeping her away from the wreck. The men pulled furiously to try to bring the boat alongside but in vain. In this critical situation one of the men aboard *Sorrento* streamed a line on a fender. It swirled to and fro in the

*A fathom is six feet so this would be 320 yards.

Kingsdown lifeboat *Sabrina*. W. Honey

eddies but at last came within reach of the bowman's boat-hook. A heavier cable was rapidly made fast, the *Sabrina* drew alongside and all forty-six men were taken off.

Heavily laden as she was, the coxswain dared not risk the lifeboat going broadside on to the seas and his only hope was to drive, with wind and sea dead aft, clean across the four miles of broken waters on the Goodwins. The Walmer boat followed and, as soon as they were clear of the breakers, came alongside to take off some of the rescued. Even this was perilous enough for she was swept in by a sea and crashed against *Sabrina's* gunwale. At last the transhipment was completed and both lifeboats luffed up as much as they could, to land the rescued men at Broadstairs.

This rescue was a fine example of seamanship and skill. Similar fine seamanship and knowledge of the Sands were displayed by Arnold's great nephew Freddie Upton in the years immediately after the Second World War when Walmer was the busiest and most renowned station in the whole of the British Isles.

Regrettably, as is so often the case with the casualties of today, seamanship on the part of some of the old-time captains was noticeably lacking. The famous Coxswain Wilds of North Deal, who won the silver medal in 1877 and second clasp to the silver in 1882, succeeded in rescuing the crew of a Canadian vessel of 1,000 tons which drove on to the outer edge of the Goodwins in 1880. It was discovered later that the captain did not have a pilot, lacked the proper charts, had failed to take soundings and had no knowledge of local navigational marks.

The *Van Kook* of North Deal was constantly called out on rescue missions in the 1870s and 80s. One such service in the great gale of 11th November, 1877 resulted in serious damage to the lifeboat despite the coxswain's undoubted skill. The Downs were crowded with vessels when the storm broke, local luggers and "cats" scurried about with spare anchors and spars and putting men aboard vessels needing help at the pumps until the weather forced them to run for shelter. Richard Roberts the second coxswain, had been at sea all day in his "cat", *Early Morn*, but finally had had to run to Margate for shelter returning to Deal by train. He had only just arrived home when there were warning guns from the Gull Lightship and flares were seen in the direction of the Brake Sands. At once he joined Coxswain Wilds in putting out in the *Van Kook* under close-reefed mizzen and double reefed storm foresail, but before they reached the Brake the vessel had broken up and vanished. While they were searching in what the coxswain described as "a tolerable nasty sea", they saw another flare. At once they went onto the other tack but almost immediately saw another ship in distress closer at hand, her decks awash and heeling so that her yard-arms touched the water. She was a French brig, the *D'Artagnan*, and her crew were apparently so scared that they could not even jump for the lifeboat. Coxswain Wilds therefore veered down on his anchor cable till they were almost touching the stern while Second Coxswain Roberts clambered onto the fore end-box, seizing the terrified Frenchmen one by one and handing them into the boat. Frequently great breakers creamed through the night, lifting the *Van Kook* and driving her with great force against the wreck's transom. Having rescued five men, although both port and starboard bows were now stove in, Wilds took his battered boat towards the original wreck, the ship that had burnt the flare, which by then was fast breaking up, surrounded by a raffle of wreckage and rigging. She was a Swedish barque *Hedvig Sophia*, and once again they dropped anchor to windward and veered down. Although the captain's wife was understandably terrified of trusting herself to the waterlogged lifeboat, they succeeded in rescuing all aboard. Both the 12 Swedes and the five French were landed safely at North Deal, just before dawn, by an exhausted but triumphant lifeboat crew. The coxswain and the second coxswain both received silver medals.

Two years later another foreign crew owed their lives to Coxswain Wilds. On 28th December, 1879 guns from the South Sand Head Lightship warned of vessels on the Sands just after 1 p.m. in a furious south-westerly gale. The wind was whipping up the crests of the breakers on the Goodwins into pillars of foam that could be seen clearly from five miles away. Coxswain Wilds launched successfully and, hoisting reefed mizzen and reefed foresail, headed for the south-east spit of the Goodwins where they could see a large barque about a mile in among the breakers. Another smaller vessel, which they sighted, disappeared as they approached, presumably lost with all hands. They were still about half a mile from the wreck when her main and mizzen masts crashed overboard.

Coxswain Wilds dropped anchor to windward and veered down on 160 fathoms of cable gradually drawing closer to the wreck which was the German ship *Leda* bound for Hamburg. Just as the throwing cane was hurled and a rope passed across, an immense sea flung the lifeboat as high as the wreck's fore-yard and as she came down her port bilge caught the bulwarks and she almost capsized. Quickly two lines were rigged across and the German crew urged to swarm over. They were very scared but were encouraged by one of their number who, it transpired, had twice before been saved from the Goodwins by the North Deal lifeboat. When the captain, the last to leave, was crossing another huge wave smothered them, and left him clinging precariously by one hand. One of the lifeboatmen, George Philpot, who was tending the ropes, reacted with quite exceptional speed and whipped a line under his legs enabling him to scramble to safety. The Goodwins were not yet conceding defeat and as the anchor cable was cut and the foresail hoisted, another wave burst the sail and sent the *Van Kook* staggering. Under jury rig she careered across the Sands amid the smother and eventually reached Deal beach safely.

In 1881 the *Van Kook* was re-named *Mary Somerville*, a name to be carried by two other boats, ON 178, built by Forrestt and ON 227, a 42 foot × 11 foot self-righter, built by Woolfe. In these the list of gallant rescues continued, and included the *Royal Arch*, the *Ganges*, a full-rigged ship where 32 were saved after the lifeboat had almost been impaled by the dolphin-striker under the bows as she veered in and the *Frederik Carl* when Coxswain Wilds was seriously injured. Richard Roberts who took over had already been awarded the silver medal, and now he won a second and a third silver clasp during his twenty-two years as coxswain. He had forty-two years service in the lifeboat in all, being concerned in the rescue of 441 lives and died at the age of ninety-five.

A wreck on the Goodwins, showing the lifeboat and the tug *Vulcan*. From a photograph by Franklin of Deal, presumably from a painting.   *W. Honey*

On nearly all his services Roberts was accompanied by Second Coxswain E. Hanger. Marsh, Adams, Pain, Stanton, May, Betts and Brown were names that often featured in the crew lists. Not all their calls took place in gale conditions, and sometimes they were able to save vessels and valuable cargoes from the clutches of the Goodwins. One such occasion was in 1889 when the *Mandalay*, sailing from Middlesborough to the River Plate, mistook her position and ran through one of the swatchways deep into the heart of the Goodwins before striking the Sands. The sailors tried to work her off by backing the yards but without success; so flares were lit, in answer to which off came the *Mary Somerville* shortly after three in the morning.

The *Mandalay* was settling deeper into the Sands and at low tide there was only a few feet of water round her. As the tide began to rise all hands, including seven lifeboatmen under Second Coxswain Hanger, turned to in an effort to save the vessel. Coxswain Roberts in the *Mary Somerville*, with his five remaining men, laid out a kedge and helped to pass a towing hawser aboard from the tug *Bantam Cock*, but efforts to refloat the ship failed and the tug went away. Early in the afternoon Stephen Penney's lugger *Champion* arrived, her crew joining in the task of jettisoning cargo; but several galley punts which had been assisting had to make for shore as the weather was turning dirty with gale force south-west winds and a heavy swell.

As darkness fell the *Champion* lay off in the swatchway, her riding light marking the deeper water. The *Mary Somerville* lay alongside the *Mandalay*. By midnight heavy seas were breaking over the deck so that work had to be stopped and hatchcovers secured. The lifeboat surged to and fro to the full scope of her cable, buried by each breaking sea, but still standing by, while the tug *Cambria*, which had arrived at nightfall, crept cautiously in through the swatchway, the Deal men securing her heavy towing hawser aboard the *Mandalay*. As high water approached the tug passed across the bows to give a pull in a different direction, her steel hawser crossing the lifeboat's cable. This was bad enough, but worse was to follow. As Roberts secured alongside the *Mandalay*, the tow-rope got beneath the lifeboat lifting her high in the air and letting her down with a crash onto the bulwarks. All was confusion as huge breakers pounded the ship, the towing-hawser snatched taut again almost capsizing the lifeboat, one of the Deal men hacked at the cable with an axe to save his comrades, other men of the *Mandalay* secured a rope from a second tug *Iona*. At this moment the *Mandalay* lifted only to thud on the Sands with increasing violence — but with the next breaker she began to move. Thudding and crunching she came clear and into the swatchway and the 35 hour struggle culminated in the vessel being brought safely to anchor in the Downs.

Shortly before Roberts retired the *Charles Dibdin*, ON 552, a 43 foot × 12 foot self-righter built by Thames Ironworks, took the place of *Mary Somerville*. She was named after the founder of the Civil Service Lifeboat Fund who, for thirty-two years, was a most energetic and successful secretary of the R.N.L.I. This famous old lifeboat was recently discovered in the Helford River in Cornwall and is being refitted by a private owner.

On 9th April, 1909 the *Charles Dibdin* joined the *Francis Forbes Barton* of Broadstairs and the *Charles and Susanna Stephens* of Ramsgate in going to the assistance of the *Mahratta* of Liverpool aground on the Goodwins. The lifeboats stood by the vessel until the next high tide, some 12 hours later, to see if she would

William (Bonny) Adams, Bowman under Richard Roberts, Coxswain North Deal 1907-1926.   *W. Honey*

Charles Dibdin (ON 552) with first rig. Sail plan was altered in 1910.   *W. Honey*

float off but she remained aground. The *Charles Dibdin* took 14 people ashore while tugs and shore boats came out to help in getting the ship off. Broadstairs and Ramsgate lifeboats then returned to harbour, but *Charles Dibdin* came out again to stand by for the second night in case she was needed. By six o'clock next evening it was considered wise for the rest of the passengers to leave and at about 9 p.m., it becoming clear she was going to break up, all except the captain and some officers were taken off. Early in the morning she broke her back and the captain and the other officers had to abandon ship. So *Charles Dibdin* with 24 rescued persons on board made for shore after an exceptionally long service of over 50 hours.

Meanwhile Walmer had a new lifeboat *Civil Service No 4*, ON 34, a 40 foot × 10 foot self-righter built by Forrestt, on service from 1884-95. She, in turn, was followed by a second *Civil Service No 4*, ON 394 of similar dimensions and built by Hansen of Cowes. This boat rescued 155 lives before the Station was temporarily closed in 1912.

Kingsdown had had the *Charles Hargrave,* a 36 foot × 9 foot self-righter built by Forrestt, on station between 1882-1890 and a second boat of the same name in 1890, ON 306, which was a larger 40 foot × 10 foot self-righter built by Woolfe.

The *Charles Dibdin* at North Deal and the *Charles Hargrave* of Kingsdown were joined from 1915-1921 by a reserve boat *Francis Forbes Barton,* previously at Broadstairs, which was under the veteran coxswain, William "Cobbler" Stanton, who had served in the North Deal boat under Wilds, Roberts and William "Bonnie" Adams. The last named came from a famous Deal lifeboat family, and he himself had fifty-two years service in "the boat" being coxswain for thirteen and a half years. He helped to save 321 lives and won the silver medal for gallantry no less than three times, as well as rewards from the governments of the U.S.A., Esthonia and Italy. Most of the services in which he played such a prominent part took place during the First World War and one of these, to the Admiralty armed trawler *De La Pole*, was of outstanding difficulty.

It was about five o'clock in the morning of 4th February, 1916, that distress rockets were seen coming from the Goodwins. At once the *Charles Dibdin* was launched but with very low tide had difficulty in clearing a wreck on the shore. At length she won clear and making all speed to the Sands found a trawler hard aground with seas breaking right over her and her bows just out of the water. Three men were forward on the forecastle clinging to a rail, eight others were in the fore rigging only just clear of the breakers raging beneath them. Further aft, like a wave-washed rock, the bridge thrust above the surface, the captain still there clinging on grimly up to his waist in water.

A tremendous sea was running as Coxswain Adams tried to work the boat in close. One of the men was washed from the rigging and efforts to save him were in vain, a line was hurled across but, afraid they might be swept overboard like their fellow, the men in the rigging dared not reach it to make fast. Luckily the lifeboat took a sudden sheer and one of the lifeboatmen flung a grapnel which held fast. With all speed the men on the fo'c's'le were dragged to safety, then those in the rigging were taken off. The captain realised that in such seas the lifeboat could not work in close enough to rescue him or even get a rope to him so he sprang overside.

Civil Service No. 4 of Walmer 1897-1912 in front of Walmer lifeboat house.   *W. Honey*

William (Cobbler) Stanton, Coxswain North Deal Reserve
boat *Francis Forbes Barton*.   *W. Honey*

Coxswain Freddie Upton, awarded silver medal for service
to the *Sylvia Onorato*.

Photograph by Norman Cavell.   R.N.L.I.

As he was swirled wildly towards them, the lifeboatmen flung a rope, it missed, but a
second line fell over his shoulders and he was dragged to safety. Then, unable to
beat back to Deal, the lifeboat made sail for Broadstairs where the rescued men were
landed, in an extremely exhausted condition.

This service, difficult as it was, was only the prelude to a far more arduous and
dangerous rescue operation in November, 1916 during the worst gale for many
years which raged from the seventeenth to the twenty-first. In 24 hours the
Ramsgate, North Deal, and Kingsdown boats saved 82 lives.

The south-south-west wind was gusting up to hurricane force and a
mountainous sea was pounding over the Goodwins when at 8 p.m. on 19th November
distress signals were seen. At that state of the tide North Deal could not launch, so a
number of men hurried over to Kingsdown where an unsuccessful attempt was made
to launch the *Charles Hargrave*. The whole position was all the more difficult
because of the large number of seamen away on war service. At about 10 p.m., when
the tide had risen sufficiently, North Deal launched and made for the Goodwins in
intense darkness and blinding rain squalls, reaching the wrecked Italian steamer
Val Salice at about midnight.

The guardship in the Downs helped by floodlighting the steamer with her
searchlight but the lifeboat had to face formidable breakers which frequently tossed
her almost to the level of the steamer's mastheads. Letting go his anchor, Coxswain

Adams veered down as close as he could but the lifeboat was sheering about wildly and no rope could have held her alongside. The only hope for the shipwrecked crew was to clamber down the side of the wreck on rope ladders and be dragged aboard the lifeboat one by one as she surged in. At last the whole crew of thirty were aboard the North Deal boat, a rescue that has been described as little short of miraculous, and thankfully the coxswain cut his anchor cable and made for Deal.

Four hours later, with the weather deteriorating another distress signal came from a large steamer that had gone aground just south of the *Val Salice*. The Deal reserve boat *Francis Forbes Barton* launched under Coxswain Stanton, in tow of a Dover tug. Twice the tow rope snapped and members of the crew were injured before she reached the scene to veer down towards the steamer *Sibiria* on her anchor cable. Conditions on the Goodwins were so frightful that she was unable to work alongside. The lifeboat was constantly filled with water, three times she almost capsized and, at the fourth attempt, she was caught by a mountainous breaking sea, flung on her beam ends so that mast and sails went under water and, as she righted herself, the mizzen mast and after thwart were carried away. With several of his crew injured Stanton had to cut the cable, give up the attempt and make for Deal. The R.N.L.I. awarded him the silver medal for his gallant and persistent efforts to effect the rescue.

Ramsgate now took up the struggle, as we have seen, and meeting the same atrocious conditions, having had a bollard wrenched clean out of the boat and several of her crew injured, was forced to turn back. All that day hurricane seas battered the *Sibiria* and in the late afternoon a further attempt to reach her was made, this time by the Kingsdown boat *Charles Hargrave* under Coxswain James Pay. He was sixty years old at the time and had been coxswain since 1910, a man of great experience and knowledge. His crew was supplemented by a dozen Deal men many of whom had already been out in one of the other boats and one, William Hoile, had been out already both in the North Deal and in the reserve boat. At length, after being knocked back up the beach and swamped, they managed to launch. A tow from a naval vessel brought them to the edge of the Goodwins, they ran in, lowered anchor and veered down on the wreck which, by this time, was awash. Giant seas were pouring over the deck, all the crew were congregated on the wrecked bridge as the lifeboat veered in closer and closer until at last she was near enough for the men to jump. One by one they were rescued, the lifeboat meanwhile filled over and over again by the breaking waves, and being flung up level with the bridge and then dropping away 18 feet below it. It was a herculean task but by 9 p.m. all 52 men were taken off, the anchor cable was cut and the *Charles Hargrave* returned triumphant to the shore.

Coxswain Pay received the silver medal for gallantry, and the President of the U.S.A. also showed his country's appreciation of this splendid rescue by monetary awards to the crew and a gold medal to the coxswain.

Only three years later the President of the United States had occasion to make another award, this time a gold watch to Coxswain William Adams of North Deal and gold medals to all members of the crew for service to the steamer *Piave* of New Jersey. She went aground with a crew of 96 on the Goodwins during a snowstorm on 29th January, 1919 and North Deal launched at about 10.30 p.m. The lifeboat stood by until tugs arrived and helped to secure towing hawsers but attempts to shift the *Piave* were unsuccessful. The lifeboatmen then joined in the work of jettisoning cargo, work which went on until the 31st. At about half past five in the evening of that day with a heavy sea running, there was a loud report from below decks. Immediately the crew prepared to abandon ship but before anyone was ready the ship heeled over on her side, the electricity failed and everything was plunged into utter darkness. In the ensuing confusion while some of the crew struggled into the lifeboat others lowered away one of the ship's boats. The after-fall tackle of this went with a run and the boat was hung up by the bows, shooting the men in her into the water. Lines were thrown and at length they were all dragged to safety in the lifeboat which now had 29 rescued on board. The Ramsgate boat was now on the scene so Coxswain Adams made for shore but soon after leaving the wreck the lifeboat was caught in a whirlpool, spinning round about 50 times before she could get clear of it and make for Deal beach. The Ramsgate boat rescued a further 23 and the remainder were picked up by the tugs.

That same October there was another fearful gale lasting three days, the wind often gusting to hurricane force, in which the North Deal lifeboat rescued two survivors from the Esthonian schooner *Toogo* after an all night search. Coxswain Adams and four members of the crew were badly injured, so that when another call came, William Stanton took out the *Charles Dibdin* rescuing two from the ketch *Corinthian*. The seas were so frightful that it took the lifeboat nearly six hours to reach the Sands. Coxswain Stanton at this time was waiting to go into hospital for a serious operation but when the doctor called he found his patient had gone afloat.

Although exhaustive tests of petrol engines had already been made all these services were still carried out by pulling and sailing boats for no motor boat could yet be launched safely down the shingle. However with the development of the Beach type motor lifeboat in the offing, the *Barbara Fleming*, ON 480, built by Thames Ironworks in 1902, which had been at Kingsdown between 1926-1927 was temporarily transferred to Walmer while North Deal and Kingsdown were closed. Finally *Charles Dibdin Civil Service No 2*, ON 762 came on station in 1933 at Walmer as the first motor lifeboat to cover the Goodwins. She was 41 foot × 12 foot 3 inch, built by Groves and Guttridge of East Cowes and gave outstanding service, rescuing 387 lives.

It was with this boat that Walmer experienced a spell of quite extraordinary activity starting with the last year of the Second World War, a spell which made the station the busiest in the British Isles and brought medal awards to Coxswain Freddie Upton and his mechanic Percy Cavell who served under four coxswains until his retirement in 1962. His wife, Mrs Julia Cavell, who was recently awarded the Gold Badge for her years of devotion to the lifeboat services comes from one of the most famous Deal lifeboat families, the Adams. Cavells, too, have long links with the Walmer lifeboat, Mr Norman Cavell having been for many years the energetic and enthusiastic Honorary Secretary of the Station Branch. In 1976 he received the singular honour of being awarded the statuette of a lifeboatman in recognition of his outstanding services in the field of public relations. Mention should also be made of Dr James Hall, who became world famous as the "Lifeboat Doctor" and was awarded the O.B.E. for his service in the boat. A memorial clock to his memory is on the landward side of the lifeboat-house.

There was a service to the Admiralty anti-submarine boat No 25, on the night of 18th January, 1944. In the rain-swept darkness the anti-submarine boat drove on to the Goodwins, not far from the East Goodwin Lightship, at full speed. The shock drove the propeller-shaft right through the ship's bottom, her engine-room caught fire but the sea poured in and put out the flames; and there she was, stuck fast, her bows sticking up and her stern right under water. Coxswain Mercer, realising the urgency of the call with the tide rising on this squally night, took the *Charles Dibdin* by the direct route across the Sands through the pounding surf. The skeletons of old wrecks made the passage doubly dangerous, but he picked them out with his searchlight and came safely across. Aboard the wrecked launch the crew of 13, soaked, exhausted and helpless had been watching the rising tide for nearly two hours knowing that in a very short time they would be engulfed. Just as it seemed that all hope was gone, they saw the groping finger of the lifeboat's searchlight. Coxswain Mercer was awarded the Bronze Medal for gallantry for this rescue.

On another occasion that same winter he stood by the trawler *Snakefly* which had stranded on the Goodwins. For six hours the lifeboat was out in mountainous

Charles Cooper Henderson launching. Haul-off warp visible alongside.   *W. Honey*

seas sustaining damage to her rudder and guard rails. The trawler was pounding wildly, heeling over on her side, then righting herself before being caught by a succession of huge seas which knocked her off the Sands. Whilst this was happening the lifeboat was close alongside, with Second Coxswain Upton aboard the trawler helping the captain prevent her going aground again while the crew dealt with a fire in the engine-room. Coals from the boiler fires had shot all over the place as she pounded clear. At last the trawler was brought to safe anchorage in the Downs but, when he came ashore Coxswain Mercer said, "I've never seen such seas in forty years or wind either. More than once I thought we had all gone." Words like these from an experienced seaman show more clearly than any description the terrible dangers our lifeboatmen face in their services on the Goodwins, even in modern motor lifeboats.

There was an astonishing series of wrecks of American Liberty Ships, starting with the *Abraham Baldwin*, aground in the ominous Trinity Bay, in 1944, from which Freddie Upton took off the entire crew of 31 in hurricane conditions.

One of the most difficult services was to the *Luray Victory*, a 9,000 ton vessel, which struck the southern most edge of the Sands on 30th January, 1946. In the cold blackness of the night the lifeboat drove through heavy surf and found her fast aground surrounded by such heavy seas that it was impossible to go alongside. The *Charles Dibdin* stood by for the rest of the night and, in the early dawn, ran a hawser out to a tug but with conditions worsening, efforts to tow her off at high tide were unsuccessful. With the prospect of another long spell of standing by, the lifeboat returned to Walmer to re-fuel and for the crew to get dry clothes and food. Away only a short time the lifeboat returned to find the situation changed.

The wind had backed to southerly and was blowing a full gale, the ebb was sluicing past the steamer's sides as she began to break up. The ship groaned and creaked, ducks bulged, derricks and masts tottered and fell while down below water trickled then spouted through the widening rents in the hull. The lifeboat worked in as close as she could but found that the furious surf and racing tide were setting up such a wild sea that no rope could hold her alongside. Also the sands beyond the stern of the vessel were beginning to dry so speed was essential if the lifeboat herself were not to become stranded. Coxswain Upton took her in, bows on and, as soon as she was near enough, the lifeboatmen snatched the crew one by one to safety from rope ladders hanging down the ship's side. In this way the whole complement of 49 men were taken off in half-an-hour.

Later the same year another American ship, the *North Eastern Victory* piled up on the South Goodwins in misty conditions. When the *Charles Dibdin* reached her, she had broken her back and the engine-room was flooded. The crew of 36 were taken off but the master decided that he and six officers would remain on board. The lifeboat reached the shore at 8.35 p.m. on Christmas Eve but as the weather was worsening she launched again to stand by throughout the night. At dawn the *North Eastern Victory* was listing and breaking up, so the master and officers were taken off and brought safely ashore on Christmas Day.

Charles Cooper Henderson caught "in the itch" on returning from service — probably winter 1972-1973.

W. Honey

Another service, perhaps the most dangerous carried out by the *Charles Dibdin*, took place early in January 1948. The weather at the time was very thick, with rain squalls and heavy wind which had been blowing for several days, just the type of weather that raises the most dangerous conditions on the Sands. As it cleared briefly, the Coastguard sighted a ship aground. Without delay the lifeboat was called out and made in her direction, finding the seas on the Sands even heavier than expected. The ship, a 2,300 ton Italian vessel, the *Sylvia Onorato* bound for Rotterdam, was hard and fast on the Sands. Coxswain Upton afterward described the seas out there as "like mountains", and it was one of these that almost brought disaster to the lifeboat. She was close alongside when suddenly one of these great mountains of water flung the *Charles Dibdin* upwards until her crew were looking down on the hatches and bridge of the stranded vessel, then broke, throwing the lifeboat straight at the wreck. With engines full astern she clawed back and as she fell a great chunk of the red rubbingstrake was ripped off as she thudded against the bulwarks. Another foot and the Goodwins might well have claimed a lifeboat and her crew.

67

Meanwhile tugs had arrived but the ship was in such a difficult position and the weather so bad that it proved impossible to get hawsers aboard. One of the lifeboatmen, Ginger Thomas, went aboard to advise the captain on how to attempt to drive the ship off with her engines but this failed. The tide fell, the seas increased in fury and the captain was advised to abandon ship, but would not do so. After standing by all night the *Charles Dibdin* returned to shore to refuel and obtain food and dry clothes for the lifeboat crew. On their return the captain still refused to leave, the *Sylvia Onorato* was still unable to work off on the next tide and the lifeboat stood by for a further night before again returning to the shore. On Sunday afternoon for a third time the weary crew put out and with reports that a south-westerly gale was imminent, the captain agreed to abandon ship. Although the task of rescue was immensely difficult, with the lifeboat surging about in the increasing seas, one by one the 28 crew, plus two German stowaways, and one large Alsatian dog were taken off successfully and brought ashore after a service lasting nearly 72 hours. The silver medal was awarded to Coxswain Upton and, for his part in the rescue, the mechanic, Percy Cavell, received the bronze medal.

Both the coxswain and mechanic were awarded bars to these medals as well as Silver Gilt medals from the French Lifeboat Society for an extremely difficult service on the night of 13th/14th January, 1952. The night was very dark, a south-westerly gale was blowing, with mist and squalls of rain. In these conditions the lifeboat was called out to the help of the 4,000 ton French steamer *Agen* which had piled up on the South Goodwin. The exact whereabouts of the wreck was uncertain and, when Freddie Upton reached the given position there was no sign of any vessel. Keeping very close to the western edge of the Sands he returned on his course. Suddenly he saw a flare on the far side of the Goodwins about a mile away, but when he tried to cut across the Sands he found the seas so tremendous that he decided he must work round the southern extremity and then northward to the wreck. He described these seas later as "standing up like a cliff".

At 2.45 a.m. the lifeboat drew near to the wreck and in the searchlight beam the coxswain could see that the ship had broken in half, the two parts being separated by about thirty feet of swirling foam. The breakers were pounding right over both parts, the crew were clustered, soaked and exhausted, up in the bows. The tide was running fast, there was a heavy confused sea, and from the broken hull jagged pieces of metal projected into the surf. It was dangerous to go alongside but several times Coxswain Upton tried it without success. He decided he must wait for conditions to improve.

A short time afterwards the wind veered westerly and moderated slightly though it was still gale force, so just after 6 a.m. he made another attempt. Because of the way the ship was lying in the Sands the only course was to go through the gap between the two parts of the ship. The tide was now low but it was still dark and the seas were heavy. But by working his engines ahead and then astern he managed to hold the lifeboat in position while 37 Frenchmen slid down into her. The captain, however, refused to leave so the coxswain, unwilling to risk the lives of those already rescued, took them ashore. Then once more he faced the dangerous trip, this time succeeding in taking the captain off, after a service which had taken 11 hours altogether.

In 1959 *Charles Dibdin, Civil Service No 32,* ON 948, a 42 foot × 12 foot 3 inch Beach type, built by William Osborne of Littlehampton, came on station to serve until 1975. The type of rescue began to change, with more services to yachts and small craft, so in 1964 an Inshore Lifeboat was stationed here as well. In its first 10 years this boat saved 89 lives and five of the enrolled crew won badges for meritorious service.

The types of service have changed but the perils remain, despite modern equipment, radio-telephone and echo-sounders. In an article Sir Herbert Russell wrote in the old *Morning Post* in 1934, "Recently I was yarning with an 80-year-old Deal boatman. His conclusion was that things have changed a mortal lot but the chaps, they are still just the same."

On 14th May, 1972, a yacht was seen burning distress flares in the vicinity of the South Goodwin Lightship and the *Charles Dibdin* was launched at 4.20 a.m. The casualty, the ketch *Nell,* agreed to fire flares to guide the lifeboat, but though sighted by the lightvessels, these were not seen aboard the lifeboat. Coxswain Henry Brown, however, picked up the yacht's radio reporting that her engine had broken down, that she was in very shallow rough water and was being driven towards wrecks. The coxswain at once realised she must be near the South Goodwin buoy, near the wreck of the *Luray Victory* so he made for the position, soon sighting a red flare ahead. Making radio contact with the casualty Coxswain Brown approached the spot, soon sighting the *Nell* being driven north-north-easterly by the gale. She was touching bottom in the troughs and was rolling heavily in the steep seas. The tide was sweeping her towards the wreck and there was no time to lose. Coxswain Brown ran in towards her side and two lifeboatmen, Norman Griffiths and Gordon Green, climbed aboard to help the crew. Three people were taken off before the furious rolling forced the coxswain to pull astern. The *Nell* was now hitting bottom so hard that her masts were shuddering. As she rolled most heavily to port, the coxswain ran in to starboard but three guard-rail stanchions were smashed as the yacht came down heavily on the lifeboat which herself touched bottom. Two more men were taken off, there being now less than 100 yards between the yacht and the wreck. The owner being reluctant to leave, a tow rope was passed and the lifeboat took the strain. For a time no progress was made as the ketch was frequently dipping her bows under and striking bottom regularly as the lifeboat's echo-sounder showed a maximum of 10 feet. In a final effort the coxswain put his engines full ahead and to everyone's surprise the tow held and the *Nell* was pulled clear of danger. For this service a vellum recording the thanks of the Institution was awarded to Coxswain Brown.

This is only a small part of the story of the Deal, Walmer and Kingsdown lifeboats. So much more could be written, such as that of the second *Mahratta* that went on to the Sands in 1939 and of the *Helena Modjeska* that piled up on the fine afternoon of 12th September, 1946, the sea oily calm. The captain refused the help of the lifeboat at first but the crew had to be taken off a few tides later as the ship snapped in two.

Now the last *Charles Dibdin* has been replaced by the *Hampshire Rose*, the result of Sir Alec Rose's appeal for funds, one of the 37½ foot × 11½ foot Rother class boats built by Osborne's, adapted for launching down the beach. She is wooden built, has 12 watertight compartments and is equipped with all the latest safety and navigational aids; and she has already added her quota to the tremendous total of well over 2,000 lives rescued by the three Deal Stations during their 120 years of lifeboat service. But for every successful rescue mission there have been dozens of other occasions when the boat has merely stood by and then at last returned to her station. Such an incident was recorded, so graphically, by John Ryan in the *Guardian* newspaper of 14th August, 1975. After nine tedious hours, waiting and watching a stranded yacht till she floated off safely, the *Hampshire Rose*, at half past one in the morning, returned to Deal "to a welcoming floodlight on top of the boat house, lined up with a hand-held light on the beach and headed straight for the recovery crew standing by the waterline. At the last moment, he wrote, "the man with the lamp leapt aside and we hit the soft shingle at speed, sliding crazily but accurately towards the slipway . . . within minutes the boat had been hauled to the turntable, turned around and set for the next launching."

The *Hampshire Rose* stands proudly on the launching ways, her bows pointing to the Goodwins. At any hour of the day or night men may be called out in all weathers to face hardship and danger in an effort to save life and to battle with the treacherous Sands. Little wonder that 19 awards for gallantry have so far been won by Deal, Walmer and Kingsdown for these men are truly heroes of the sea.

Naming ceremony of the *Hampshire Rose* 1975.   *Author's collection*

CHAPTER FOUR

THE DOVER STRAITS

Dover, Folkestone and Hythe

CONDITIONS at the eastern entrance of Dover harbour, at 10.30 p.m. on 1st December, 1975, were appalling, the storm force wind against tide creating a confusion of breaking seas so frightful that the Dover lifeboat *Faithful Forester* lay right over on her beam ends as she cleared the breakwaters. The 44 foot Waveney had just been called to the assistance of the 1,199 ton Cypriot coaster *Primrose*, adrift with steering gear trouble, and now she headed through the roaring night in a 70 knot hurricane.

Two Townsend ferries *Free Enterprise VII* and *Free Enterprise VIII* reached the scene, and just before 11 p.m. the *Primrose* reported that she had rigged a jury rudder which gave her some steerage. By 11.20 p.m. the Dover lifeboat also reached the casualty, guided by a searchlight from *Free Enterprise VIII*. She had battled through the mountainous seas from the harbour mouth at an average speed of over 7 knots in spite of the conditions, the waves running well over 25 feet high. It was a fine piece of seamanship on the part of Coxswain Lidden to reach the scene so rapidly and now he took up position close to the casualty, standing by in case of need.

Some idea of the fury of that night can be gathered from the report of the captain of *Free Enterprise VII* in which he said, "The weather at this time was the worst I have experienced in this area in some eighteen years service in the Dover Straits, my anemometer was indicating 100 m.p.h. in regular gusts and then settling at 70 m.p.h. Had Admiral Sir Francis Beaufort lived 170 years later he would certainly have had second thoughts on his wind scale."

In the midst of all this smother came an extraordinary link with the old days of sail when the training ship *Malcolm Miller* came driving under bare poles* toward the casualty. Fortunately the warning broadcast on V.H.F. by *Free Enterprise VII* made it possible for avoiding action to be taken in time.

During one of the heavy 100 m.p.h. gusts the violence of the sea and wind was such that the *Faithful Forester* was again laid right over on her beam ends. Anyone who has been in a boat forced over like this by sheer wind power will know the anxious moments whilst she wavers as if deciding whether to turn over or recover. In the case of *Faithful Forester* she was laid over for a full half minute before the gust eased and she righted herself.

All this time the coaster was being driven slowly north-eastward but as the tide slackened the wind dropped slightly to some 60 m.p.h. The coxswain advised the *Primrose* to bear up to the west to gain some shelter from the land. This sound advice brought the coaster safely to within two miles of Dover Harbour but when

---

*In a recent letter to the *Lifeboat Journal* one of the crew on that occasion wrote that they were carrying a foresail and a storm mizzen.

Dover lifeboat *Sir William Hillary* 1930-1940. Special fast motor lifeboat 64 foot × 14 foot built by John I. Thornycroft.   *R.N.L.I.*

she asked for a pilot it was impossible for the cutter to put out. Coxswain Lidden offered to guide her in and by twelve minutes past four she was safely within the harbour from which no other vessel had been able to leave throughout the night.

Captain Robinson of the *Free Enterprise VII* said later, "The whole incident from start to finish must be the finest piece of seamanship I have ever seen with such limited facilities in the worst possible conditions and I salute that small band of dedicated lifeboatmen who risked life and limb for some eight hours."

The silver medal for gallantry was awarded to Coxswain/Mechanic Arthur Lidden, the bronze medal to Second Coxswain Anthony G. Hawkins, and the Thanks of the Institution on vellum to Assistant Mechanic Richard J. Hawkins, and Lifeboatmen John Smith and Gordon Davis.

This service gives an idea of the furious seas that can rush through the Straits of Dover, seas that have caused problems of silting in the harbour from earliest times. When the Roman pharos on Castle Hill flared its beacon fire to guide the galleys into Portus Dubris, and when the Saxons and Normans used the place as the main gateway to and from the continent there was always this problem of the fast flowing tide moving shingle and silt into the bay. At first the main harbour area was right beneath the great Norman fortress which has frowned for centuries over the haven and welcomed home the returning traveller. Then it was moved much further westward in an effort to beat the shingle. Tolls were levied on shipping in 1474 and 1481 to enable the town walls and harbour to be repaired, and a pier was built running out from the western beach. Henry VIII took a keen interest in the problem but Camden wrote, "The town is more noted for the convenience of its harbour (though it has but little of that left it) and the passage from thence to France, than either its neatness or populousness."

In 1676 the old custom was revived of requiring every townsman on the beating of a drum to go down to the harbour armed with a shovel to clear shingle. Thomas Digges was foremost in the work of building a flushing sluice to disperse the bar by using the dammed up water of the River Dour, a method only partially successful.

Further work in the eighteenth and nineteenth centuries was more effective but not until the Admiralty pier was finished in 1871, jutting right out into the tideway, was an efficient answer found.

Despite all these centuries of difficulty, Dover as one of the principal ports of the Cinque Ports federation was always a military and naval base as well as the great route to the Continent. Henry III ordained that no one should cross the channel to any port but Dover, and pilgrims were forbidden to leave England from any other port. These regulations were understandably profitable to the town and there were many notable arrivals including Henry V on his return from his victorious campaigns and Charles II returning to his kingdom at the Restoration. The London to Dover road, the old Watling Street of the Romans, was the regular stagecoach route, the fore-runner of the "iron road" of the London, Chatham and Dover Railway which attracted custom by excursion return tickets to Dover at 2/6d. In the early Victorian times families flocked here for seaside holidays. With all this incessant traffic it was appropriate that the Dover Humane Society should have stationed a lifeboat here, at Townsend, as early as 1837. She was a 37 foot × 7 foot 9 inches boat built, to a local design, by Elvin of Dover but there are no details available of her name, service launches or lives saved during the 16 years of her service.

In 1853 she was followed by another unnamed boat supplied by the Dover Humane Society and built by T. C. Clarkson of London.

This boat is of particular interest as it was the result of a prototype, 25 foot in length which had been tested at Dover in 1852. The boat was built of "Clarkson's patent material" which was a laminate of alternate layers of canvas, cork and wood, having high end boxes to provide self-righting capability. The Dover Humane Society was so impressed by its performance that they ordered a 28 foot × 7 foot 6 inch version which was duly tested at Woolwich and delivered to Dover in 1853. In 1855 when the Dover Humane Society asked the R.N.L.I. to take over the station she was altered to Peake's design and resumed her station, but in 1857 she was withdrawn from service, returned to her builder, and purchased by Miss Burdett Coutts.

What happened to her is not certain. It seems probable, however, that she was sent to Sunderland and another boat, incorporating Clarkson's air-cases, was given by Miss Burdett Coutts to the boatmen of Margate.

The R.N.L.I. now provided a new boat, a 28 foot × 6 foot self-righter built by Forrestt pulling six oars, which was in use from 1858-1864. Despite the increasing volume of cross-channel traffic she appears to have had only one service launch.

From 1837 right up to the First World War, the lifeboat was kept on the beach nearly opposite the monument and launched by horse and manpower. With the advent of first the steam and then the internal combustion engined boats they were moved to what is known as "the camber" at the eastern end of the harbour where they were kept afloat.

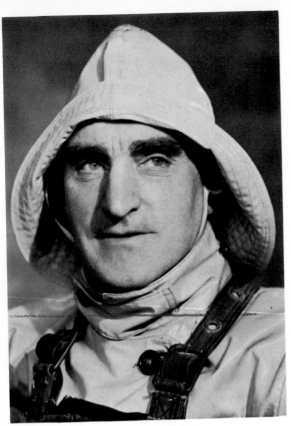

Coxswain John Walker.
Photograph by Lambert Weston of Dover.   *R.N.L.I.*

Coxswain/Mechanic Arthur Lidden.   *R.N.L.I.*

The fourth lifeboat was the *Royal Wiltshire*, a 32 foot × 7 foot 5 inch boat, pulling ten oars and built by Forrestt, which came on station in 1864 and with her began a notable record of life-saving missions. It was in her that the famous Coxswain J. Woodgate began his long spell of twenty-four years in command of local lifeboats.

The first medal award, that of a silver medal, was awarded to Major H. Scott on the occasion of the service to the barque *Chin Chin* on 2nd February, 1882. The *Royal Wiltshire* was replaced by the *Henry William Pickersgill*, a 35 foot × 9 foot self-righter built by Woolfe, which was on station between 1878 and 1888. Her number of service launches was only eight before she herself was replaced by the *Lewis Morice*, ON 197, a larger heavier boat, built by Henderson, 37 foot × 8 foot and pulling twelve oars, which had a far more active spell of duty being launched 17 times in the course of which 31 lives were saved. It was while this boat was on station that Coxswain Woodgate was awarded the silver medal for gallantry in December 1891 and again he received a bar to the silver medal in 1893. The first was possibly for his efforts to reach the *Benvenue*, the second perhaps connected with his astonishing rescue of the crew of the Norwegian barque *Johannes Marie* after thirty hours at sea.

In 1901, a new 37 foot × 9 foot 3 inch self-righter, built by Thames Ironworks and pulling twelve oars came into service, the *Mary Hamer Hoyle*, ON 461, and it was this boat that launched to the aid of the s.s. *Olaus Olsson* of Stockholm on 20th October, 1906. At this time yet a further extension to the Admiralty Pier was being undertaken and this Swedish timber boat collided violently with the new works at about 11 p.m. being severely damaged. The signal to summon the lifeboat crew was immediately given and *Mary Hamer Hoyle* was afloat and on the way to the casualty in 11 minutes, a marvellously quick launch in the circumstances, the crew having to assemble and the boat to be man-handled into the water across the beach.

She continued here right up to the outbreak of the First World War when, with the port such an important naval base for the Dover Patrol, the lifeboat station was closed, and remained so until a steam lifeboat, the *James Stevens No 3* came on station in 1919 and remained on service for three years.

These steam lifeboats were of particular interest in that the first of them, the

Tanker *Sovac Radiant* ashore near South Foreland, January 1952. Lifeboat *Southern Africa* assisting.
Photography by Graphic Photo Union. R.N.L.I.

Duke of Northumberland which was built at Blackwall by J. and F. Green, was powered by water jets — a revolutionary idea then but one which would not seem out of place today. She made a trial trip up the Thames to Syon House, and was then given extensive service tests in the course of which it was found that she could get up steam from cold in 20 to 23 minutes. She was a heavy boat, 50 foot × 14 foot 3 inch weighing 30 tons, and had to have a technical crew of four but proved herself a fine seaboat. The Prince of Wales, later King Edward VII, who once said of the lifeboat service that "it was one of the finest and noblest to which a human being can belong", took a particular interest in the development of this boat as did his nephew, the Kaiser. Other steamers followed, three jet-propelled in all, but in 1898 two were ordered from J. Samuel White of Cowes fitted with screws in specially designed tunnels to protect the propeller blades. These tunnels were similar to those in use in modern motor lifeboats.

The two White steamboats, *James Stevens No 3* and *James Stevens No 4*, were in service in 1899. They were 56 foot 6 inch × 14 foot 8 inch drawing 3 foot 6 inch and with twin funnels side by side. *James Stevens No 3*, ON 420, went first to Grimsby, next to Gorleston where she gave excellent service and then on to Milford Haven and it was this boat that re-opened the Dover station after the war. However during her three years she was only launched on service five times and then the station was closed again. It had seemed unnecessary to have a lifeboat here as well as at the neighbouring harbour of Folkestone, especially since the upkeep costs of the steamer, over £800 a year, were particularly heavy at that time.

Meanwhile, in addition to the regular cross-channel steamers from both Dover and Folkestone which had started operations as long ago as 1861, a new form of transport was soon to make its mark. Blériot had flown the Channel in 1909 and by the later years of the First World War Sopwith Camels, de Havillands, Vickers Vimys and Bristols had seen service over the Western Front. The daring pilots who handled those cumbersome machines or who engaged in aerial dog-fights with von Richthofen's "circus" were soon able to find employment with Imperial Airways when they were demobbed. Sir Alan Cobham and other pioneers were zealous in promoting interest in flying, and a "trip" across to Paris by air heralded the stream of flights that cleave the skies today. The R.N.L.I. was fully aware of this surge toward aviation so special steps were taken.

Folkestone lifeboat had been having relatively few calls, so Dover was reopened yet again, this time with the world's fastest lifeboat principally designed to rescue "ditched" airmen. Launched on 22nd November, 1929 from Thornycroft's Hampton-on-Thames yard, she had a length of 64 feet, a beam of 14 feet and a draught of 4 foot 9 inches. Double skins of teak on oak timbers with steel bulkheads forming 8 watertight compartments made a staunch boat, the two 12 cylinder Thornycroft engines developed 375 bhp giving a speed of 17 knots. This splendid boat came on station in January 1930 bearing the name of the founder of the R.N.L.I., *Sir William Hillary* and in ten years was responsible for rescuing 29 lives while service launches reached the remarkable total of 45.

During the Second World War *Sir William Hillary* was sold to the Admiralty who were eager to use such a fast and sturdy boat and once more the station was closed until, at length, *J. B. Proudfoot*, ON 690, became the Dover lifeboat in 1947. This 45 foot × 12 foot 6 inch Watson, built by J. Samuel White in 1924, had already seen years of service at Cromer under the famous Coxswain Henry Blogg as well as being the reserve boat at Margate which had rescued pilot officer Richard Hillary during the war. Now she continued her tale of service launches when on the morning of 28th June, 1947, she set out into the fog in response to wireless signals for help from the steamer *Heron* of Piraeus. This ship had been in collision with the Danish vessel *Stal* and had sunk some 14 miles east-south-east of Dungeness. The Walmer lifeboat *Charles Dibdin* had also launched but had later been recalled when it was learned that the survivors had been picked up by the British motor ship *Suavity* which was heading for Dover. The *J. B. Proudfoot* met her about two miles off Dover, the 23 survivors and the pilot were transferred and duly landed together with a ship's boat just after noon.

A strange service occurred during the morning of 21st August, 1948. There was a strong southerly breeze and a very rough sea when the s.s. *Baron Eliban* reported sighting two men in a rowing boat east by south of Dover. The lifeboat put out, rescued the exhausted men and, on her way back, also took in tow the yacht *Salamat Jalan* which was unable to make harbour in the heavy seas. On arrival in harbour it was found that the two men in the rowing boat had stolen it, so they were handed over to the police.

The *J. B. Proudfoot* was replaced by the *Southern Africa*, ON 860, a 52 foot × 13 foot 6 inch Barnett lifeboat built by Rowhedge Ironworks and presented by the

Hythe lifeboat *Mayer de Rothschild* in 1891. *Hythe Archives*

Wreck of the *Benvenue* off Seabrook, November 1891.   *Hythe Archives*

Southern Africa branch of the R.N.L.I. and a great spurt of activity began for this station. In only 18 years 263 service launches were recorded and she has easily the largest record of lives saved, a total of 186.

A serious incident occurred in September 1951. One very dark night with heavy squalls Coxswain John Walker was on the Eastern Harbour arm when he sighted a small yacht, the *Akeco* of Amsterdam, anchored just outside the arm. She was less than half a mile from shore and her anchor was dragging. He hurried back to call out the lifeboat and at 11.45 p.m., without waiting for the last two crew members, *Southern Africa* put out. The gale against ebbing tide and the rebound of the waves from the cliffs and the harbour arm caused a violent and dangerous maelstrom of breaking seas. When Coxswain Walker reached the yacht, he found her broadside on to the wind and seas, within 30 yards of the cliffs and right among huge rocks and boulders, some of which were only just covered by breaking seas. In appalling conditions he managed to lay the *Southern Africa* alongside, the whole scene illuminated by his searchlight, a rope was thrown and made fast, and steadily the lifeboat drew the yacht clear of danger.

Although such a short service, both boats entering harbour some 45 minutes after the lifeboat launched, it was splendid seamanship. The slightest error of judgement on the part of the coxswain must have resulted in both boats being dashed to pieces on the rocks by the mountainous waves. Coxswain John Walker was awarded the bronze medal for gallantry for this service.

Another service which illustrates the many ways in which lifeboats assist ships in distress occurred in January 1952. The large Panamanian tanker *Sovac Radiant* went aground near the South Foreland and at about half past ten at night the *Southern Africa* put out to her aid. A strong south-south-west gale was blowing, kicking up a very rough sea and as the crew of the tanker were in no immediate danger the lifeboat stood by. Early next morning she passed a line across from a tug, but heavy seas were now breaking over the tanker and the line parted. A second line also carried away, but a third held. Towards dawn more tugs arrived.

The lifeboat was kept busy taking soundings, guiding the tugs to suitable positions where they could exert their pull in the right direction but without endangering themselves. Meanwhile it was reported that a pilot boat, *June Rose*, had fouled her propeller, and when dawn came she was found to be right on top of some of the towing hawsers. The lifeboat managed to haul her clear, towed her into the harbour and then returned to the tanker which refloated about noon. It was largely due to the help of the lifeboat and the skill and seamanship of the lifeboat crew that this valuable tanker was saved.

In August 1952 came the *Western Farmer* service when the *Southern Africa* joined the Ramsgate lifeboat, picking up the doctor from Walmer on the way. When they reached the *Western Farmer* they found the ship already beginning to break up, and the crew taking to the boats. The *Southern Africa* picked up 13 men who were in the second ship's lifeboat and were in grave danger of drifting onto the capsized fore-end of the wreck, while Ramsgate rescued the remainder.

Sometimes even calm seas require seamanship of the highest order as on the 24th May, 1953. That night the channel was shrouded in the thickest fog, in the midst of which the *Andaman* of Gothenburg was in collision with the Panamanian steamer *Fortune*. Shortly after 3 a.m. the lifeboat set out and headed through the dense fog, in response to wireless messages from the *Andaman* reporting that she was sinking and her crew of 38 were taking to the boats.

No-one who has not experienced the baffling nature of thick fog at sea can have the slightest idea of the strain involved in searching for drifting boats. When darkness is added to the grey blindness of the mist the task becomes harder still. Presently a message came through that the s.s. *Arthur Wright* had picked up the survivors and at 5 a.m. the lifeboat managed to find this vessel and take them aboard. It gives some idea of the difficulties of the service when one realises it was not until 8.45 a.m. that the *Southern Africa* was back on her moorings.

One of the most interesting features of this station is the "pen" or dock in which the lifeboat is moored, and the way in which the crew, scattered and employed in a wide variety of trades, is collected in case of emergency. When the alarm is given the station van speeds off to collect the men at certain fixed points along the road whilst others arrive by their own personal transport. On arrival they enter the loft where protective clothing and life-jackets are ready for use, from there they swarm down the steps into the boat; within a few minutes of the maroon the lifeboat is under way.

Crew swinging down into the lifeboat from the mizzen rigging of *Benvenue*.

Drawing in The Illustrated London News.   *Hythe Archives*

1956 was a notable year for the crew of the *Southern Africa*. The lifeboat was returning from a special visit to the South Goodwin Lightship in November in connection with a B.B.C. television programme when she picked up distress signals from a helpless fishing boat. So television viewers were able to share the thrill of a real rescue in the wind-lashed Straits.

Earlier that same year Coxswain John Walker was awarded a bar to his bronze medal for the rescue of ten people from the yachts *Towi*, *Sonia* and *Madame Pompadour*. The wind was hurricane force, with gusts up to 80 knots kicking up a stormy and confused sea.

A service on 12th November, 1961 was of extreme danger and discomfort in the reserve lifeboat, a 45½ foot × 12½ foot Watson named *Cunard*, then on temporary duty at Dover. A message at 9.49 p.m. the day before had reported that the East Goodwin Lightship had broken adrift so the Walmer lifeboat launched but by the time she reached the lightvessel the crew had managed to let go an emergency anchor and the ship was riding safely. By midnight the wind was storm Force 10 and there was such a rough and confused sea that the lifeboat could not stay alongside but had to circle the lightship throughout the night. In the morning it was arranged that she should be relieved by the Dover lifeboat, so the *Cunard* stood by in appalling conditions for 12 hours until she in turn was relieved by Ramsgate. Fortunately the lightship's anchor held and weather conditions presently moderated so that the Trinity House tender *Vestal* could re-secure her in position.

A further lightship service occurred on 2nd December, 1966 when, in a storm force south-westerly wind, the Varne lightvessel was reported out of position. The Trinity House vessel *Siren* put out but conditions were too bad for her to move the lightship, and her commander asked the Dover lifeboat, *Southern Africa*, to stand by in case the lightship dragged nearer the Varne bank. Coxswain Cadman found the lightship pitching and rolling heavily and sheering wildly about in waves up to 20 foot high and with the wind swinging into the west the *Siren's* commander asked the coxswain to take the crew off. At 10.42 a.m. the lifeboat made her first run in, five of the men being taken off; the lifeboat backing away after each man had jumped and then coming in again for another run. On the fifth run a porthole was broken aboard the lightship. Finally the last crew member and the master were taken off safely by 11.35 a.m. and the *Southern Africa* returned through the storm to Dover. A letter of commendation was sent to Coxswain A. E. W. Cadman D.S.M. and the crew of the lifeboat for this arduous and skilful service.

In 1967 after her long spell of duty here, *Southern Africa* was replaced by the third of the 44 foot × 12 foot Waveney class of steel lifeboats built by Brooke Marine of Lowestoft, the *Faithful Forester*, the result of a generous gift from the Ancient Order of Foresters. After her naming by Princess Marina, Duchess of Kent,* her two 215 h.p. diesels sprang into action and she sped out into the outer harbour for a short trip watched over by the Walmer lifeboat *Charles Dibdin*. So once again Dover has a new fast lifeboat, the stability and manoeuvrability of which is so well exemplified by the service mentioned at the beginning of this chapter. In

*This was Princess Marina's last naming ceremony in Kent. The Duke of Kent, Princess Marina's husband, was President of the R.N.L.I. from 1936 to 1942; she herself succeeded as President in 1943 to 1968 when her son, the Duke of Kent, became President in 1969.

her first nine years she has launched on service 151 times saving 143 lives, and with her advent the Dover Straits area right out to the Varne lightvessel was most effectively covered.

Twelve R.N.L.I. gallantry medals have been awarded to Dover boatmen, five silver and seven bronze, a fine record for this famous seaport.

The sister station of Folkestone was established in 1893 at a time when Dover already had her sixth lifeboat on station. This fine seaside town, with its hotels and spreading beaches forming five miles of seafront, has grown up alongside a very old established fishing harbour, which King John used as a naval base. Later it became a port for the South Eastern Railway Company's fleet of cross-channel steamers which started operations in 1861. In addition the passenger tug *Conqueror* and other early paddlers made the trip from Margate or Ramsgate round to Folkestone.

Folkestone also has a particular place in the history of the R.N.L.I. for the first lifeboat, the pulling and sailing boat *J. McConnel Hussey*, ON 343 built by Ellis of Lowestoft, which was here till 1903, was one of the first boats chosen to be fitted with a petrol engine. She was a 38 foot self-righter and was launched on service only four times saving ten lives.

When equipped with a 2-stroke Fay and Bowen 9 h.p. motor the trials at Newhaven during 1904-1905 were very promising, the boat attaining a speed of six knots. Her stability was thoroughly tested and found to be quite unaltered, and her self-righting capability was undiminished. She was then transferred to Tynemouth where Captain Burton R.E., was the leading spirit. He was an enthusiastic engineer, and when the local crew refused to have anything to do with this new-fangled boat, he enrolled a volunteer crew to man her and affected a successful rescue. As a result of this the regular crew agreed to serve in the boat so long as Captain Burton was there to superintend the engine.

Folkestone meanwhile received a new self-righter, *Leslie*, ON 508, 35 foot × 8 foot 6 inch pulling ten oars built by Thames Ironworks, which was on service between 1903 and 1930. During the First World War and again from 1922 to 1929 she was covering the Dover area when that station was closed; but with the arrival of the fast lifeboat *Sir William Hillary* to reopen the Dover station and with a motor lifeboat at Hythe the need for the Folkestone station no longer existed and it was closed.

Among the most meritorious services at this station was the service to the fishing smack *Good Intent*. On 5th October, 1904 there was a violent south-westerly gale and the lifeboat was called to the aid of the smack which was in difficulties in the high seas. So furious were the waves that the *Leslie* was caught and flung up the beach time and again, but the crew and helpers ashore struggled undaunted to get her off. At last they succeeded but two members of the crew were washed out of the boat and mercifully picked up again. After dropping anchor to windward of the smack, the *Leslie* veered down and the three members of the crew were taken off shortly before the vessel drove ashore on the rocks where she was dashed to pieces. A great crowd witnessed the safe return of the lifeboat even though it was 2.30 a.m.

The silver medal for gallantry was awarded to Coxswain Stephen Cook for his courage and determination in effecting this rescue.

Earlier that same year Coxswain Cook and his crew were involved in an extremely long service to the s.s. *Marzo* of Bilbao which had been holed in a collision in fog. She was beached in a sinking condition where, with the lifeboatmen assisting, the holes were patched and finally, refloating on the rising tide, she was towed by tug to Dover. The *Leslie* did not return to her station till 8 p.m. the next day, over 24 hours after she had launched.

With the decline of coastwise sailing craft which might get into difficulties in the bay between the South Foreland and Dungeness the number of services declined, but it is a measure of the skill and courage of Folkestone seamen that five silver medals were awarded by the R.N.L.I. although all but one of these were to Coastguards before the opening of the Lifeboat Station.

Hythe, only a few miles from Folkestone, is also now closed as the area can be effectively covered by the Dover and Dungeness lifeboats. Between 1876 and 1940 there were 76 launches on service in the course of which 66 lives were rescued and a fine record of five silver medals and one bronze were won by the men of Hythe. The station was closed with the loss of the motor lifeboat *Viscountess Wakefield* in 1940 when she was taken across to Dunkirk, manned by naval ratings, and out of 19 lifeboats on this historic rescue mission she was the only one lost.

The pleasant little town, hemmed in by the hills that shut Romney Marsh off from the "mainland" of Kent, has a long history as one of the Cinque Ports, its quota to that fleet being five ships each manned by 22 men and a boy. It tends to

Folkestone/Hythe lifeboat crew who carried out the rescue from *Benvenue*. Wright Griggs second from right, back row. Coxswain Hennessey on left of front row, Thomas Shelley next to him, Second Coxswain Sadler second from right. *F. C. Shelley*

spread sideways in the direction of Dymchurch and the great shingle beach has robbed it of all capacity as a port, nor is there much evidence today of its ancient importance. In a guide-book of 1803 quoted by Teignmouth Shore it is described in these terms:

"Hythe has long been the resort of invalids, for the purpose of bathing; and a considerable number of convenient lodging-houses have been recently built for the accommodation of visitors. They are, in general, upon a small scale; but in the season, the company if not so numerous here as at some of the watering places upon this coast, is as genteel and more select, and of late years much improved by the families of many military officers of rank, permanently or occasionally stationed in the vicinity . . ."

This reference makes one aware of the considerable military importance of this place at the time of the Napoleonic wars. Rifle and firing ranges, the Hythe school of musketry, Martello towers which spread along the Dymchurch wall, and above all the Royal Military Canal built by William Pitt the younger as a defensive work to prevent French invaders from streaming into the hinterland of Kent, serve as reminders that the sea and the watchers of this coast have been our shield for many a long year. Today the remaining watchers are reinforced by the electronic eyes of radar which can see further and in conditions of fog and darkness.

Hythe has, moreover, a very special interest to those interested in the history of the lifeboat service, for, as we have seen, Lionel Lukin, the inventor of the "un-immergible boat", is buried in the local churchyard.

The first lifeboat house was built at Seabrook to the east of Hythe and the first lifeboat came on station in 1876. She was the *Mayer de Rothschild*, ON 58, a 35 foot × 9 foot self-righter built by Woolfe, which stayed here until 1884, and made five service launches. She was followed by a second *Mayer de Rothschild*, ON 35, a 37 foot × 8 foot self-righter, pulling 12 oars, and also built by Woolfe. It was in her that Coxswain L. Hennessey won the silver medal for gallantry for the service to the ship *Benvenue* of Glasgow in November, 1891.

This was an epic rescue in hurricane seas. The *Benvenue*, which had been under tow, broke adrift and striking the bottom sank about 300 yards from the shore off Seabrook. All those aboard lashed themselves in the mizzen rigging but the captain and four hands were soon swept away. Ashore frantic efforts were being made to rescue the survivors and the Dover lifeboat launched but could not reach the wreck. Lawrence Hennessey, who had already rescued four Frenchmen from the schooner *Eider* ashore at Hythe at great risk to himself, now tried to launch the lifeboat from Sandgate but she was flung back on the shore. At noon he tried again from Hythe but the boat overturned in the breakers and, bruised and exhausted, he helped to drag his men to safety but, in spite of all efforts, one was lost. Efforts by the 52 Battery, Royal Field Artillery, to shoot a line aboard failed. At 9 p.m. Coxswain Hennessey managed to launch successfully and took off the 27 survivors who were landed at Folkestone. As the boat was overloaded several of the

Special medal awarded for the *Benvenue* rescue to Thomas Shelley.

Reproduced by courtesy of his son, F. C. Shelley

lifeboatmen hung on to the lifelines overboard on the homeward leg. Queen Victoria was so impressed by the display of dedication by the lifeboat service that she granted permission for her profile to be on a special medal struck to mark this gallant rescue and awarded to each member of the crew. Hennessey was awarded the Albert Medal 2nd class and Second Coxswain Sadler received the silver medal of the R.N.L.I.

Altogether the second *Mayer de Rothschild* launched 20 times on service, rescuing 27 lives. She was then followed by a third lifeboat of the same name, ON 610, built by Thames Ironworks, 35 foot × 5½ foot and 10 oars. By this time a new lifeboat house had been built at the western end of the promenade where she was housed between 1910 and 1929. Among her 14 launches was one that shows particular skill and determination in very rough weather. The 72 ton ketch *Mazeppa* of Harwich anchored in Hythe Bay just after midnight on 1st April, 1917, but by 2.30 a.m. in the morning she was dragging her anchors and driving on to the shore.

Watch had been kept on the vessel as local seamen feared she might be in trouble in that position and in such a gale, so distress flares were seen immediately they were fired and the lifeboat launched to her aid. Only with the utmost difficulty could the lifeboat close with the ketch for the waves were piling up into a confusion of breaking seas but at last she managed to veer down on her anchor cable and approach near enough for ropes to be thrown. One man sprang over from the *Mazeppa* with a line fast round him and was hauled to safety in to the lifeboat. Then she had to stand off as the fury of the surf made it impossible to remain near the wreck.

A short while later she veered down again and the other man aboard was dragged to safety. The cable was cut and the lifeboat returned to shore after a most difficult service in a full gale. Coxswain J. Dearman was awarded the bronze medal, and so was Second Coxswain Wright Griggs.

Another dramatic service, performed with the utmost skill and daring, took place just twelve years later, on the evening of 11th November, 1929.

At 6.30 p.m. with a 70 mile an hour gale blowing, the coxswain at Hythe, H. A. ("Buller") Griggs the son of Wright Griggs, received news from Dungeness that a barge, the *Marie May* of Rochester, had broken from her moorings and was drifting to leeward. At about 8 o'clock, when the wind had risen to hurricane force, Coxswain Griggs saw a light about four miles away and, later on, red flares. His crew stood by and he called up Dungeness which was the weather boat or lifeboat upwind of the flares. Dungeness launched but only with the most incredible difficulty. In the blinding rain-squalls Coxswain Oiller searched in vain, only discovering the barge at daybreak by which time Hythe had rescued the crew.

All this while Coxswain Griggs had kept watch and, seeing flares still being fired at about 3 a.m. and no sign of the Dungeness boat, he decided to launch. The *Mayer de Rothschild* had the utmost difficulty in getting away in face of the mountainous seas, but at last she was off and two hours later found the barge in the surf only about a quarter of a mile from the shore. With great skill and daring Coxswain Griggs managed to manoeuvre alongside and lines were put aboard by which the three men of the crew were saved. The rescue came only just in time for they were utterly exhausted and the barge already had well over a foot of water in the hold.

For their very gallant rescue in the face of extraordinary difficulties, and for his judgment in taking control of the situation in the absence of the Honorary Secretary, the silver medal was awarded to Coxswain Griggs. The bronze medal was awarded to Coxswain Oiller of Dungeness for his dogged courage in launching in the face of such terrific seas and staying out until he found the barge.

With a record of 14 launches and 14 lives saved the third *Mayer de Rothschild* was withdrawn in 1929, and her place was taken by a 35½ foot × 8 foot 10 inch self-righting motor lifeboat built by Saunders Roe of Cowes, the *City of Nottingham*, ON 726. With the neighbouring station of Folkestone closed she saw 17 service launches in the six years she was on station and was responsible for saving 16 lives. One of these services in 1934 was to a motor boat the *May Belle* which had got into difficulties off Littlestone. With her engine broken down she began to drift in the strong south-westerly wind in a rough sea. On receipt of the news from the Coastguard the *City of Nottingham* launched to the rescue, finding the *May Belle* right in shore to windward of a groyne. Three of her passengers had managed to swim and struggle to shore, but the lifeboat veered down on her anchor, put a line aboard and contrived to tow the motor-boat clear rescuing the other three occupants. This was a comparatively short service but was carried out with great skill and judgement in awkward conditions close to the shore.

Again the same year the *City of Nottingham* was called out in thick fog with a strong north-easterly wind to a vessel ashore near Copt Point between Hythe and Folkestone. At first it was thought to be a cross-channel steamer and the *Sir William Hillary* launched from Dover but returned to port on hearing that the steamer had reached Folkestone safely. The *City of Nottingham* meanwhile had difficulty in getting away as a rope had fouled her propeller but at length she located the vessel in trouble which proved to be the Royal Fleet Auxiliary *Argo*. Running alongside, the coxswain went aboard to assist the master in the necessary preparations for floating off. The lifeboat continued to stand by while tugs put two ropes aboard, the vessel refloated safely on the rising tide and escorted by the lifeboat, she made for Dover. The *City of Nottingham* was finally back at her station at 1.45 p.m. after being out for seven hours.

In 1936 the *City of Nottingham* was withdrawn and sent to Clovelly where she served till 1949. Her place at Hythe was taken by the *Viscountess Wakefield*, ON 783, a 41 foot × 12 foot 3 inch beach type lifeboat, weighing 14 tons and built by Groves and Guttridge of Cowes, which was on station until 1940 when she was lost at Dunkirk and the station was closed.

These are only a few of the services carried out from Hythe but they will serve to give some idea of the dangers faced by the crews of the lifeboats there and of their fine record of skill and seamanship.

City of Nottingham launching from the beach at Hythe.

Photograph by Express Photos Ltd. R.N.L.I.

CHAPTER FIVE

OFF DYMCHURCH WALL

New Romney, Littlestone and Dungeness

THE strange flat land of Romney Marsh stretches to the south of Hythe and its towns are rich in history. At Dymchurch the "Lords of the Levels" still hold authority to deal with the incursions of the sea and further south lies the ancient Cinque Port town of New Romney.

Here, where now lie spreading fields, a notable port once flourished, from which ships sailed to join Harold's fleet against the Norman invader and, in 1347, four ships from here crossed to the siege of Calais. Although the sea has receded, there still remains a nautical flavour to Romney and as late as the fourteenth century ships could moor alongside the churchyard. Later many a cargo of smuggled goods was landed on the marsh, a fact which formed the setting for Russell Thorndike's famous novel, *Dr Syn*, a name now carried by an engine on the miniature Romney, Hythe and Dymchurch Railway.

With this seafaring background it was only fitting that when one of the Dungeness lifeboats, the *Providence*, was moved to Littlestone in 1861, the station should be given the name of New Romney. The record of launches between its inception and closure in 1928 is 76, in the course of which 121 lives were saved, four of these from the ketch *Speculator* of Jersey. In addition to this fine record one gold medal and one silver were won by men of New Romney and the King of Sweden made special awards of silver medals to all members of the crews of the New Romney and Dungeness boats after the service to the brigantine *Aeolus* of Arendal in November 1891.

Ten years after the establishment of the station a new lifeboat was given by Mrs Jane Hatton, the *Dr Hatton*, 32 foot × 7½ feet and built by Woolfe, and she also provided for the erection of a new lifeboat house. After rescuing 32 lives this boat was replaced by the *Sandal Magna*, ON 36, the gift of Mr Joseph Spawforth, in 1884.

This lifeboat, a 34 foot 7 inch × 7½ foot self-righter built by Woolfe, seems to have been the busiest of the five boats stationed here. Launched on service 24 times in 16 years, a total of 47 lives were rescued by her though losses were suffered among the gallant crew who manned her. In 1891, the *Sandal Magna* was launched at night in the midst of a terrible snowstorm and capsized. Three of the crew were drowned, but the remainder were found by the coastguards, chilled and exhausted, in the vicinity of End House, Littlestone. In spite of this disaster, the lifeboat was ready to put out to the aid of the Swedish ship *Aeolus* on 11th November later that year, a day of bitter wind and raging sea when no less than three vessels were in distress off Littlestone. The Dungeness boat was also launched to the *Aeolus* but

Funeral parade outside Littlestone lifeboat house of three members of crew of New Romney lifeboat *Sandal Magna*, and crews of schooners *Echo* and *Hugh Barclay* who lost their lives 9th March, 1891. *Photograph supplied by A. E. Turner of New Romney*

capsized with the loss of two of her crew, but the *Sandal Magna* managed to reach the wreck and succeeded in rescuing her crew of eight.

November seems to have been a particularly busy time for the *Sandal Magna*, for in that month two years later she was involved in a lengthy and arduous service to a Norwegian barque, the *Johanna Marie*. *Sandal Magna*, the Hythe lifeboat, *Mayer de Rothschild*, the Dover boat *Lewis Morice* under Coxswain Woodgate and a tug all answered the call but so terrible were the conditions that not one of them was able to get alongside. The lifeboat crews, with the courage and endurance so typical of these very gallant men, would not admit defeat. At last, after 26 hectic hours, the Dover boat managed to veer alongside the wreck and take off all the crew.

After capsizing yet again, fortunately without casualties, the *Sandal Magna* was replaced by the *James Stevens No 11*, ON 438, a 35 foot × 8½ foot self-righter, pulling ten oars and built by Thames Ironworks, one of 20 lifeboats presented to the Institution by Mr James Stevens of Birmingham.

About midnight on the 23rd March, 1904 the Coastguards reported signals of distress off Littlestone Point. It was a cold wet night with a strong north-easterly gale and rough sea, but the *James Stevens* launched successfully and, once clear of the breakers, bore down on the vessel, the *Antje* of Geestemunde. She found the seas breaking right over her and the crew in great danger. She therefore pulled in under her lee-side and the five men managed to jump to safety. The lifeboat then returned to its station and managed to beach safely, with the aid of helpers ashore, despite the very heavy surf.

Another of her services was to the master of a ship in a most unusual and dangerous position. On 8th January, 1909 information was received that the master of the *Malpas Belle* of Truro, beached the previous day at Littlestone in a leaking condition, was making signals of distress. The *James Stevens* launched and on reaching the vessel found that she was being swept fore and aft by the waves. Afraid that the mast might go overboard the master had clambered to the end of the bowsprit where he was clinging on desperately. The lifeboat managed to work in close enough for him to leap down into the boat, and he was brought safely ashore.

After serving for twelve years the *James Stevens* was replaced by the *Henry Wright Russell*, ON 630, 35 foot × 8½ foot and built by Thames Ironworks, which was on station until 1928, but during her spell of duty only three service launches were recorded. So with the number of calls becoming less and less, it was decided to close the station, the area being effectively covered by Hythe and Dungeness and, since 1947, by Dover and Dungeness.

The old slip at Littlestone Point, New Romney was demolished for security reasons during the last war, and the old boat house was removed. The location was marked by a seat, made from the timbers of the old lifeboat house and presented by Major Teichman-Derville. The enthusiasm and keenness of the local financial branch, in promoting the work of the R.N.L.I., keeps in mind the gallant service given by those who manned these lifeboats in days gone by.

An Inshore Lifeboat Station was established at Littlestone in 1966 and this boat already has a considerable record of service, being launched 180 times and rescuing 125 persons in its first ten years.

Further along the coast is the extraordinary nose of land where the lifeboat-house of Dungeness stands proudly above a bank of shingle where a keen fresh wind always blows. One feels very far out in the channel and it is quite uncanny, from the roadway, to see the hull of some vast tanker rising, apparently, almost alongside the shingle ridge. There is always the incessant beat of ships' engines, a strange steady drone blending with the snarl and rasp of the waves tugging at the shifting shingle. Relics of war-time army huts, asbestos bungalows, and the low stone and weather-boarded cottages of the fishermen crouch on this great platform of shingle, concrete paths lead to the cottage doors whilst the massive bulky shapes of the nuclear power-stations and the new pencil-thin lighthouse break the skyline.

Standing in the lifeboat-house and gazing down the launching-ways to the amazing view of the ever-restless sea one realises the problems of launching from such an exposed position.

The station here was founded in 1826 and in 1976 it celebrated its 150th anniversary, a vellum being presented to mark the occasion. A lifeboat, 20 foot × 6¾ foot built by Plenty of Newbury and pulling six oars was here, near Tower 27, Dymchurch, between 1826 and 1836 manned by Coastguards who were awarded one gold and two silver medals. She was replaced by a 25 foot boat, built by Harton of Limehouse in 1833, which was in service between 1836 and 1839 but after this there seems to have been an interval till 1853.

There followed a third boat, 27 foot × 7½ foot built by Forrestt to Peake's design, from 1854 to 1856 and a fourth, 28 foot × 6 foot also built by Forrestt, from

1857 to 1861 which seems to have been involved in a remarkable capsize in 1858. In October of that year, this small six oared self-righter with a crew of eight Coastguards put out in a heavy sea to a wreck which appeared to have been abandoned by her crew. As she was returning to shore she was struck violently by a wave, broached to and capsized flinging the men into the water. Luckily as she swung over, the anchor and its cable flew out, brought up the boat and the crew, wearing lifejackets, scrambled back aboard and reached the shore safely. It was this boat that was later moved to Kingsgate and given the name *Brave Robert Shedden*. During this time further silver medals were awarded to the gallant Coastguards manning these boats for their rescues from the *Melsomene*, the *Louise Emilie* in 1853 and the *Caroline* of Norway in 1859. It was not only the Coastguards who were honoured for, in 1867, the gold medal was awarded to the Reverend Charles Cobb, M.A., Rector of Dymchurch, for plunging into the gale-whipped seas and hauling to safety a helpless man from the rigging of the French lugger *Courrier de Dieppe*. The new Coastguard buildings at Dungeness have been named Charles Cobb Terrace in his memory.

The next lifeboat, *Providence*, a 30 foot by 7 foot self-righter by Forrestt, which had such a fine record of service, saving 49 lives, was moved to New Romney as their first boat in 1861. Dungeness station was closed until 1874 when the *David Hulett* arrived, launching from the neighbourhood of the present lifeboat house until 1887. She was again built by Forrestt, a self-righter of 33 foot × 7 foot 5 inch pulling ten oars, and during this time she was launched on service 15 times and rescued 27 lives.

This was the time when the number of R.N.L.I. stations was increasing steadily as a result of the remarkable growth of casualties around the coasts of the United Kingdom. In 1872 the total casualties were 2,381 but by 1902 this had risen to an alarming figure of 4,124. In 1872 the number of all lifeboats was 233, and the lives saved 569. Year by year the lifeboat fleet grew until it reached its maximum in 1895 with a total of 308 boats. The R.N.L.I. has always been ready to re-assess the need for stations and around the turn of the century the small-vessel carrying trade declined and, as was stated in the annual report of August 1905, steam and well-found vessels had taken its place. The fishing industry had also undergone changes and where it had died out it became desirable to close stations, or else shift them to more suitable positions. Thus by 1903 the total number of boats had gone down slightly to 289.

This again was the reason for the re-opening of Dungeness which quickly became one of the busiest stations in the southern Dover Straits, even having a second lifeboat stationed there from 1892 to 1938. The story of Dungeness is also closely linked with the fishing community and, like many other lifeboats, has a very strong connection with certain families, especially as, with such a relatively small community, all the men and women join in the work of launching the boat. In earlier times boys would rush to assist in turning the capstan to bring the boat back up the skids, dreaming of the day when they might become members of the crew,

Women launchers of Dungeness in front of lifeboat *R.A.O.B.* 1894-1912.
Standing, left to right: Miss Lottie Tart, Mrs Deer, Miss Madge Tart, Mrs Rebecca Tart (Mrs Serena Fair's mother), Mrs Welfare, Miss Annie Tart. Seated, Left to right: Miss Nellie Tart (Doris' mother), Miss Dorothy Tart, Miss Amelia Tart.

regarding the coxswain with the sort of veneration nowadays more often reserved, with far less justification, for "pop" stars.

With the arrival of the *David Hulett* on station, the fisherfolk took over the manning of the lifeboat from the Coastguards. At first there was some rivalry between them, a legacy of the times when illicit cargoes were run, but gradually suspicion was overcome and replaced by the mutual respect that still exists today.

Among the families with long connections with the lifeboats, the Tarts and Oillers are outstanding. Long before the time of the French Revolution, when religious toleration was not even considered, the Tartes, who were Huguenot fishermen, crossed the channel to seek freedom from persecution. Many of them settled at Dungeness and here they were joined by the Oillers who hailed from Cornwall. These two families have played a leading role in the story of the Dungeness station and well before the turn of the century there were Tarts and Oillers as officers of the boats, to say nothing of the many others who helped to launch her.

The problems of launching have always been very great at Dungeness where the contour of the shingle bank is altered with every tide. Ben Tart who was coxswain for ten years up to 1974 kept in his mind the tide changes and the state of the shingle every day so that, if the call came, he would know exactly how and when the boat could launch. The launchers too, have to bear in mind the effect of wind and tide so that they can lay the skids over which the boat will run at the correct angle to launch her safely. Many of these launchers are ex-crew members and the women of Dungeness have long been famous for turning out with the men to drag the skids into place.

The *RAOB*, ON 130, which took over from the *David Hulett*, was presented to the Institution by the Royal Antediluvian Order of Buffaloes. Built by Forrestt, a 34 foot × 7 foot 6 inches self-righter pulling ten oars, it was this boat that was involved, with the *Sandal Magna* of New Romney on a service to the Swedish brig *Aeolus* of Arendal when she was stranded on 11th November, 1891. Whereas the *Sandal Magna* succeeded in rescuing the eight men, the *RAOB* capsized with the loss of two lifeboatmen. Coxswain J. Lucas was awarded the silver medal for gallantry for his seamanship and courage in launching to the *Aeolus* and the King of Sweden awarded special silver medals to all members of the crews of both lifeboats. It was after this that it was decided to form No. 2 Station equipped with an additional and heavier boat. Among those receiving this award was Isaac Bonguarde Tart, whose two sons Fred and Bill also became members of the crew. Doris Oiller, ex-Coxswain Ben Tart's wife, was Isaac's granddaughter on her mother's side.

The *RAOB* continued to experience severe difficulties in launching owing to her weight, which was over three tons, and again in 1893 she capsized on service, one of her crew being lost. As a result she was withdrawn after 11 service launches during which 20 lives were saved. Her place was taken by a special boat designed by Felix Rubie who was appointed Assistant Surveyor to the R.N.L.I. in 1894, and Chief Surveyor in 1906.

Crew of Dungeness lifeboat, (c. 1910), about the same date.
Standing, back row: third from left; "Uncle Bill" Tart (Ben's grandfather), 5, 6 and 7; Fred and Bill Tart and Peter Oiller. Standing, front row left to right: Charles Oiller (Doris' grandfather), William Thomas (Peter's grandfather), Old Jackner Oiller, Jack "Chokum" Oiller, Tom Richard Tart (Ben's father). Seated, left to right: George "Wener" Tart (George's father), Jack Brignall, Alfred Tart, John Pope, Charles Williams, Douglas Oiller (Doris' father).

Charles Cooper Henderson 41 foot × 12 foot 3 inch Beach type, coming ashore 1933.
Photograph by The Times. R.N.L.I.

Rubie who had been a keen sailor at Cowes, was apprenticed in naval architecture with Denny of Dumbarton; and he now designed a boat with the particular needs of Dungeness in mind. She was of similar size, 34 foot × 8 foot, had bulkheads of specially treated canvas, and also air-cases of the same material in her double bottom; as a result her weight was only 1 ton 17 cwt. This boat, *RAOB*, ON 374, again presented by the Order of Buffaloes and also built by Forrestt, came on station in 1894 and was involved in no less than 53 launches in her 18 years at Dungeness. Robin Tart, the second coxswain, was succeeded by Arthur Tart in 1897, Charles Oiller was a member of the crew and William "Uncle Bill" Tart was head launcher. No lives were lost from *RAOB*, ON 374, despite her large number of services.

In addition to this very light lifeboat, the much larger *Thomas Simcox*, ON 312, a 44 foot × 11 foot self-righter pulling 12 oars weighing 9 tons and built by Woolfe, was supplied for the No. 2 station. Her spell of duty 1892-1915 covering much the same period as the *RAOB*, ON 374, her total of 24 service launches added to those of the *RAOB*, indicate the extreme importance and activity of this station.

Many of the services by these boats were to vessels damaged by collision and some were of extraordinary duration, among them that to the s.s. *Lake Michigan* in February 1904. The *Lake Michigan* was a large steamer of over 9,000 tons bound from St John's, New Brunswick to London. She had a general cargo including a number of cattle and was involved in collision at half past three in the morning with an unidentified sailing vessel. She was badly holed and the fires in her boilers were soon swamped but her captain just had enough steam to beach her. The *Thomas Simcox* launched at 5.30 a.m. and stood by the vessel until the following night in a rough sea when some of the cattle men wanted to land. There was also a tug in attendance and they transferred to her but, as the weather was too rough for the tug to land them, the *RAOB*, ON 374, came out to take off the 46 men. The crew of the *Thomas Simcox* who had been ashore for a brief respite now put out again to stand by in case of need and continued to do so until the evening of the 21st. By this time they were utterly exhausted so Winchelsea took over. Next morning the *Thomas Simcox* put out again, standing by until the steamer was successfully repaired and refloated on the 25th.

On 8th September of the same year at 3 a.m. the Coastguard reported distress signals and the *RAOB*, ON 374, launched into a west-south-westerly gale to find the fishing lugger *St Louise* of Boulogne with five foot of water in her hold and leaking badly. The coxswain went aboard and, despite certain language difficulties, managed to persuade her skipper to beach and then took the eight man crew off. Although filled at high tide, the leaks were effectively stopped at low water and tugs were able to take the *St Louise* round to Folkestone for repair.

In December 1906 an unusual rescue took place which provides a wonderful example of the initiative and courage which the men of Dungeness bring to bear in trying to rescue those in distress. At ten past four on the Boxing Day morning the Coastguards sighted distress signals and the *Thomas Simcox* was launched in a blinding snowstorm. They found that the ship in distress, the schooner *Ringleader* of Penzance, had already sunk and her crew had taken to the rigging. Over and over again the lifeboat tried to get alongside but furious waves and the scour of the tide swept them away. At last they were able to come close enough to the wreck for a line to be thrown but the shipwrecked men were so numbed with cold that they could do nothing. Five of the launchers on shore put off in a 16 foot fishing boat from further along the shingle and managed to work alongside the weather rigging, pulling the men into their boat and transferring them to the lifeboat.

In 1909 came an arduous service involving both boats when two vessels collided in dense fog. The cruiser H.M.S. *Sappho* struck another vessel also, curiously enough, named *Sappho*, and her position was so serious that distress signals were made and the greater part of the crew took to the boats. *RAOB*, ON 374, was launched very smartly and the captain asked the coxswain to land as many sailors as possible and to send messages to the Admiralty and Dover. With the larger boat *Thomas Simcox* now standing by, the coxswain of *RAOB*, ON 374, landed 21 and escorted the laden ships' boats to safety. She returned to assist until tugs arrived from Dover and it was decided to try to tow the warship there with a skeleton crew still aboard, one tug alongside pumping and the two lifeboats in attendance in case the watertight bulkheads gave. At last Dover harbour was reached safely and the cruiser was beached, after which an Admiralty tug towed the two lifeboats back to their stations.

Three years later the *RAOB*, ON 374, was replaced by the *Mary Theresa Boileau*, another Rubie self-righter, 34 foot × 8 foot, ON 635, built by Thames Ironworks, which remained on station until 1939. *RAOB* went into reserve and later became the boarding boat, or tender, at Walton-on-the-Naze. Although *Mary Theresa Boileau* was launched on service 24 times, the number of lives saved was only seven and before long she was joined by the heavy self-righter *David Barclay of Tottenham*, ON 644. She was started by Thames Ironworks but completed by Saunders Roe of Cowes and was a 42 foot × 11 foot 4 inch self-righter launched down skids. During her time on station Douglas Oiller, (Doris Tart's father) achieved his fine record of thirty-one years as coxswain.

Chief among his many gallant services was the one to the barge *Marie May* of Rochester on 11th November, 1929, in which both the Hythe and Dungeness boats were involved. At half past six in the evening with a strong south-westerly gale blowing up to 70 miles an hour the barge parted her moorings and went drifting to leeward with her three man crew aboard. Douglas Oiller called up the Hythe coxswain as it seemed likely that she might be blown ashore there but for some time neither coxswain knew what had happened to her. About 9 p.m. red flares were seen off Dymchurch so Douglas Oiller agreed to launch. This was an operation of the utmost difficulty as the hurricane force wind was whipping up a furious sea at Dungeness and several times the boat was slewed round in the surf but the lifeboat crew and the launchers refused to be beaten. By going right out into the undertow the launchers managed to get her away at about 10.30 p.m. after which the lifeboat began to search for the barge off Dymchurch in the area from which the flares had come. As there was no sign of her Coxswain Oiller worked out to seaward in tremendous seas, signalling the Trinity House Pilot boat on station there for information. From her he received further bearings of the flares and as a result took the lifeboat right into the shallow water close to the shore continuing the desperate search in blinding rain squalls. Still there was no sign, so signals were made but without any response at all. By this time conditions were so bad that he decided to anchor. It was about 1 o'clock in the morning and the driving spray and heavy rain made it impossible to make contact with anyone ashore. The launchers, the wives and families of the crew waited anxiously as so often before on the wind and rain-swept shingle only aware that the boat was still somewhere at sea. However by about 5 a.m. the wind veered to the north-west, and moderated slightly, so Coxswain Oiller determined to renew the search. At daybreak he and his chilled and exhausted men sighted the barge and by this time the crew had been rescued successfully by the Hythe boat. So after a service lasting eleven hours, the Dungeness boat returned to her station at about 9.30 a.m. The R.N.L.I. awarded the bronze medal for gallantry to Coxswain Oiller for his seamanship and determination in launching and continuing the search in what the Honorary Secretary at Dungeness described as one of the worst gales he had ever known; and each member of the crew received the thanks of the R.N.L.I. inscribed on vellum.

Only three years later the London barge *Shamrock* was in difficulties in a full gale and on this occasion the fury of the wind was such that the *David Barclay* was caught by a sudden gust and blown off the skids on to the loose shingle. The 37 launchers of whom 14 were women, with the wives and sisters of the crew, managed to haul her up again by the windlass, a task which Ben Tart remembers used to take two hours. Then away she went again, the skids now re-positioned, and slipping and stumbling in the loose stones the launchers got the boat away successfully. The women of Dungeness were accorded the special thanks of the Institution for their gallant services on this occasion. The women launchers of Dungeness have a fame all their own, and in 1952 Ben Tart's mother, Mrs Ellen Tart, was presented with the gold badge for fifty years service as a launcher. The same year Doris Tart's aunt, Miss Mabel Tart, was awarded the gold badge for fifty years service, and the bar to the gold badge in 1963 for sixty years as a launcher. Miss Madge Tart, also an aunt of Doris Tart and sister of the Honorary Secretary, in 1964, having helped for over sixty years, was awarded the gold badge and bar and Mrs Serena Fair, daughter of Mrs Rebecca Tart, is another holder of the gold badge for fifty years as a launcher.

It was during Douglas Oiller's spell as coxswain that the old pulling and sailing boats were replaced by the first Beach motor lifeboat, the *Charles Cooper Henderson*, ON 761, built by Groves and Guttridge with dimensions of 41 foot × 12 foot 3 inch, and at once the number of service calls rose astonishingly. In her twenty-five years on station from 1933 to 1957 she undertook no fewer than 171 launches on service, though many of these were to yachts or assisting vessels damaged in collision.

The fishing vessel *Undaunted* with engine broken down was towed back to Rye in March 1947, in August 1948 the yacht *Kestrel* of Rye was towed to the roadstead in a rough sea, the yacht *Anemone III* of Bosham was also helped to the roadstead and both crews taken off. In May 1950 it was a collision between the s.s. *Cabo Espertel* of Seville and the *Felspar* of Glasgow, the former vessel sinking. Taking off the Spanish crew from the *Fulham* of London which had picked them up, *Charles Cooper Henderson* then helped to steer the *Felspar* to Sandwich Bay.

Women launchers at work. Note skids in foreground.   *R.N.L.I.*

Doris and Ben Tart.   *Photograph by Kent Messenger.   R.N.L.I.*

Douglas Oiller continued as coxswain until 1947 when he was succeeded by
George Tart. He had began to help in launching the lifeboat during the First World
War and was very keen to get into the boat. So too was his cousin Ben Tart who
joined the crew in 1938 and became second coxswain in 1947. The importance of
the two families was emphasised by the official board of 1947 which recorded
Honorary Secretary A. L. Tart, Coxswain G. Tart, Second Coxswain T. R. Tart,
and Motor Mechanic A. J. R. Oiller.

Towards the end of the *Charles Cooper Henderson's* spell of service George
Tart won the bronze medal of the R.N.L.I. for gallantry, for the rescue of nine men
from the collier *Teeswood*.

About mid-day on 29th July, 1956 the wind was blowing up to Force 12. As it
was the last week-end in July many yachts and pleasure craft were caught out in this
great channel gale and the R.N.L.I. experienced its busiest 24 hours on record, 107
lives altogether being rescued during that time. In the twelve hours between noon
and midnight on Sunday the 29th, the *Charles Cooper Henderson* launched three
times, the first and most difficult service being to the *Teeswood*.

This motor vessel was running before the gale about four miles east of
Dungeness, trying to seek shelter when one exceptionally large sea made her broach
to. The cargo shifted and she sent out Mayday calls asking for urgent assistance.
Immediately the *Charles Cooper Henderson* launched, but by the time she reached
the position the *Teeswood* had capsized. In the huge waves and with driving rain
and spray they found a small B.P. tanker, the *B.P. Distributor*, standing by, with six
men alongside her in a raft and other survivors struggling in the water. It was
difficult to locate these men under such appalling conditions, and to hoist them into

the lifeboat, with their clothing sodden and heavy, with the boat reeling madly was exhausting work. Crew member W. Thomas tried to revive one man by one and a half hours' artificial respiration during which he and his patient were being washed about the deck by the heavy seas. While the lifeboat was in the midst of a group of survivors her propeller became snagged up by wreckage and she was momentarily adrift. With great presence of mind and skill Alexander Oiller, the motor mechanic, uncoupled the shaft and cleared the obstruction by turning it forward and back by hand. At last after about four hours and with all the survivors on board, the lifeboat began to thrust her way back to Dungeness. Coxswain Tart said, "It took us a long time to get back pounding against wind and sea." Not only did the coxswain receive the bronze medal for this service but also the thanks of the R.N.L.I. on vellum were awarded to the motor mechanic and W. Thomas. Also in the crew at the time of that service was Acting Second Coxswain Albert Haines (now coxswain), Acting Bowman Frederick Richardson, Assistant Mechanic Sydney Oiller, and crew members John Thomas, Robert Tart and Arthur Oiller. And for all of them this was one of those services that make membership of the crew so worth while. As George Tart says, "The real satisfaction of being in the crew comes when you really know that you have saved somebody, when you rescue people from the water, or when the ship goes down just after you get there. It comes when you know that there would be no other chance of their being rescued if the lifeboat was not there."

There is a strange sequel to this rescue for one of the men saved was Albert Bird, the present coxswain at Aberdeen, who was awarded the silver medal for gallantry in 1975 and it was his experience of being rescued from the *Teeswood* which decided him to join the lifeboat service.

After saving 63 lives in her 25 years on station the *Charles Cooper Henderson* was replaced by the *Mabel E. Holland*, ON 937, a 42 foot × 12 foot 3 inch motor lifeboat of the Beach type built by Osborne's of Littlehampton. With the latest equipment providing radio-telephone contact with the shore there is no longer the agonising waiting for the launchers, but there can still be difficult problems in launching a 17 ton boat like this from the beach. She is divided into 10 water-tight compartments, given additional buoyancy by 160 air-cases fitted into the hull, and her twin 48 h.p. Gardner diesels are in a water-tight engine room. Unlike the old pulling and sailing boats which required a crew of 15, she only has eight and can take about 70 survivors. A later addition has been the enclosed wheel-house and she carries an echo-sounder, searchlight and is lit throughout by electricity.

She, too, has had a tremendous total of launches though again many are the result of collisions in fog, while others have been to yachts and small craft in difficulties through engine failure. On 1st January, 1959, for example, at 10.12 p.m. the Fairlight Coastguard sighted two flares to the south-east on a stormy, overcast night with frequent squalls and at 11.05 p.m. George Tart heard a distant message on his wireless. The *Mabel E. Holland* launched and, after a search, found the house-boat *Petrina* with four people aboard, whose engine had broken down.

Naming of *Mabel E. Holland* 1957, crew of boat.
Left to right: John Oiller, Fred Richardson, Ben Tart, James Tart, Robert Tart, Jack Oiller, John Thomas, Coxswain George Tart, Arthur Oiller, Albert Haines (coxswain after Ben Tart), R.N.L.I. District Engineer in background.   *R.N.L.I.*

The Dungeness boat took her in tow with the Hastings lifeboat standing by and, in spite of the tow-rope parting once, pulled her to a safe anchorage.

Again in 1964 it was another boat with a broken down engine though on this occasion the sea was only moderate. The *Mabel E. Holland* found the fishing boat *Sea Adventure* leaking badly and towed her to Dymchurch.

In 1965 George's cousin, Ben Tart, took over as coxswain and the tale of service launches was continued.

On 27th June, 1966 she put to sea at 7.30 a.m. in a gale force west-south-west wind and a very rough sea to a yacht, the *Idle Moment*, which was only about 150 yards offshore near Denge Marsh. The two crew were taken aboard the lifeboat and lifeboatmen manned the craft which was towed to safety in Folkestone with the *Mabel E. Holland* back on station at 8.30 p.m.

In 1967 Bob Tart retired after fourteen years in the crew, Frederick Richardson after sixteen years, and Edwin Fair after sixteen years in the crew and thirty-two and three-quarter years as winchman.

Since joining the crew in 1938 Ben Tart had seen every sort of service and it was a fitting climax to the family's connection with the lifeboat that 1974, the year the R.N.L.I. celebrated its 150th anniversary, should also be the year when the last Tart in the lifeboat should win the silver medal of the Institution. Ben Tart's enthusiasm for the lifeboat service and pride in its achievements is only matched by those of his wife. He once said, "The R.N.L.I. is a wonderful organisation. They give you the best, and then it's up to you."

It was indeed up to them, coxswain, crew-members and launchers on the evening of 11th February, 1974. The wind was south-south-westerly and of hurricane force when news came that the M.V. *Merc Texco* had a badly injured man on board who needed to be landed. The *Mabel E. Holland* launched at 4.58 p.m., the seas breaking on the beach so heavily that the launchers had to be roped together as they placed the skids in case they were washed away in the undertow. As she reached the water's edge the lifeboat was between the waves and stuck in the shingle. The next heavy sea slewed her round broadside on but then, as it ran back, swung her stern out. The engines were put astern and she was starting to draw away when the next enormous wave flung her round again. As the launchers stood by as near to the water's edge as they could get, ready to re-connect the winch wire, the undertow swung her head out and Coxswain Tart was at last able to get her away. To quote the coxswain's own words in an interview with Joan Davies and printed in the R.N.L.I. journal, *The Lifeboat*, "If you ask anyone down here they will tell you that it was the worst weather that the Dungeness lifeboat has ever launched in, in living memory. And I don't fancy it would have been done in an old sailing boat — you just couldn't have got away from the beach."

As course was set for the *Merc Texco* the coxswain found that it was uncanny to steer the boat. To quote his words again, "I would say that the top 3 feet of water were going along with the wind. It was very confused and there wasn't any weight on the wheel. You couldn't feel anything. It was strange, I think there was air in the water . . . Because you could actually turn the wheel over with your little finger."

When the lifeboat neared the *Merc Texco* at 5.28 p.m. she signalled her to follow her closer inshore as the seas were enormous, but she seemed unable to do this. The wind was now well over 70 knots and the seas running 50 to 60 foot high. The ship was stopped but rolling heavily, so the first-aider Peter Thomas volunteered to try to board her. "This is where young Peter did such a marvellous job in jumping aboard. He had to watch his chance and when the ship rolled down on us he made a jump and grabbed onto the rails and our boys gave him a push and he was aboard. When the ship rolled right down her deck came nearly down to ours, then when she rolled back again, you got half the bottom up . . ."

The stretcher was passed and the coxswain decided to lie off until the patient was ready to be lowered before he ran in again, concentrating on keeping the boat as close as he could. All the crew stood ready and, as the ship lurched down towards them, they put out their arms to grab the stretcher. At last when they had the injured man safely aboard, he was taken to the cabin and strapped down with three of the crew to hold him steady. All this was done in the darkness which made it all the more difficult. Ben Tart's simple comment, "It was a lovely job. It went fine. We were lucky," only serves to emphasize the dangers of this hazardous enterprise. "It's not only judgement," he added, "you've got to have some luck when you do these jobs, or the Lord on your side."

When the lifeboat reached the shore the seas were tremendous. The shore helpers, Doris Tart among them, half hoped that they would not try to run in. Let Ben Tart finish the story, "I said to 'Honker', our second coxswain, 'What do you think about it? Think we can make it? What do you suggest?' 'It's up to you,' he says, 'You do what you think.' So I says, 'Right, if nobody don't mind, then in we're going.'" At 7.28 p.m. she was back ashore and the patient handed over to the doctor and the ambulance men.

For this service in appalling weather conditions the silver medal for gallantry was awarded to Coxswain Ben Tart, the bronze medal to Peter Thomas and the

Thanks of the Institution, inscribed on vellum, to Second Coxswain Albert Haines, Motor Mechanic Alec Clements and crew members William Richardson, Colin Haines and Arthur Oiller. The Thanks of the Institution on vellum were also awarded to "The Launchers and Shore Helpers" for their efficiency and dedication to duty in the worst beach conditions ever experienced at Dungeness.

It was a great scene in the Town Hall at Lydd on 13th February, 1975 when all the lifeboat people of Dungeness and Romney Marsh gathered for the presentation of the vellums by the Mayor of Lydd, in the presence of the Chairman of the Committee of Management and other prominent representatives of the R.N.L.I. Members of all the old lifeboat families were there in strength, and the special vellum for the launchers was received by Mrs Serena Fair, holder of the gold badge for fifty years' service. It was a wonderful occasion with, as the report says, "a table of home-baked refreshments down the middle of the hall, and so much to talk about". Among the impromptu speeches was one from Ben Tart in which he said, "When I go up to get my medal, I will not feel it belongs to me more than to anyone else in the crew. As I see it, the R.N.L.I. has recognised the service we, the whole crew, did that day by giving me a silver medal".

The *Mabel E. Holland* will soon be replaced by a new Rother class boat, Coxswain Alfred Haines has taken over from Ben Tart, new works are to be done to make the launch off the beach more possible but whenever the call comes it is certain that the people of Dungeness will send their boat out with the same courage and devotion as has always been shown throughout the one hundred and fifty years of the station and exemplified by the *Merc Texco* service.

Mabel E. Holland beaching. This gives a clear idea of the ever-shifting shingle beach.
Ian Macdonald photograph.   R.N.L.I.

CHAPTER SIX

RYE BAY

Winchelsea and Hastings

THE ancient towns of Rye and Winchelsea were part of the Cinque Ports confederation and stand on small hills which rise above the large, low flat marsh of the area. Both are rich in history particularly that concerned with men, ships and the sea. Both places have suffered severely from attack from across the channel and the onslaught of the sea. Holinshed records of Winchelsea that in 1250 "besides the hurt that was done in bridges, mills, breaks and banks, there were 300 houses and some churches drowned with the high rising of the water course".

What finally sealed old Winchelsea's fate was the appalling storm of 1278 when the place was entirely shattered, after which Edward I in 1280 made arrangements for building an entirely new town on Iham hill, laid out in a regular chess-board pattern. With a good harbour to seaward of it, the new town enjoyed remarkable prosperity providing the largest number of ships of any of the Cinque Ports at the time that Gervase Alard was Admiral of the Cinque Port fleet in 1300, and enjoyed a great trade in the export of grain and wool. Defensive walls and ditches were constructed — one reminder of which is the Strand Gate which used to lead down to the quay but which now looks over the flats of the River Brede to the fellow town of Rye. However, by the middle of the sixteenth century the harbour, which had once been the busiest on the channel coast, had silted up and by 1587 it is recorded that there were "no ships, captains, or mariners".

With the decline of Winchelsea, Rye in turn became a principal port for the crossing to France. Like Winchelsea it suffered many attacks from the French and although walled and bastioned by Edward III it was sacked in 1339 and again in 1373, 1385 and 1448. The town nevertheless survived to provide the attractive tourist centre that it is today, with the top of the hill crowned by the noble parish church of St Mary Virgin. In the reign of Elizabeth I, the same alteration in the coast line that had blocked Winchelsea harbour was already having its effect at Rye, but the town was able to play a noble part through its vessels in the defeat of the Spanish Armada. By the early seventeenth century Rye Harbour had declined, the continental trade gone with only a small amount of boat-building and Rye Bay trawlers as reminders of its maritime history. By now even these have shrunk and the picturesque Rye barges, which used to navigate the waters of the Rother, Brede and Tillingham with their great lugsails, are just a memory.

The toughness, individuality and courage of the fishermen who won their living from the waters of Rye Bay provided just the qualities needed for manning the early lifeboats. Rye and Newhaven are the oldest lifeboat stations on the Sussex coast, both of them dating back to 1803. The first boat stationed at Rye was a Greathead boat but the number of service launches made by it is unknown.

The chance of vessels being embayed or driven on to a lee shore in this bight of land between Dungeness and Fairlight was so considerable that local subscription in 1833 raised the £58 necessary for a new boat to be built for the R.N.L.I. Rye Station by Harton of Limehouse. The needs of the fishing community were uppermost in people's minds for the Rye Bay area was known for its large harvest of plaice, sole, brill and turbot. Even as late as 1905 there were between 30 and 40 smacks working out of Rye Harbour, as well as three steam trawlers. This lifeboat was a 25 foot × 5 foot 9 inch boat pulling six oars and weighing 18 cwt. She went out on service in 1852 to the brig *Avon* of London rescuing the crew of three and thus starting the fine known record of life-saving at Rye.

The R.N.L.I. transferred the third of the Dungeness boats to Rye in 1856 where she served until 1861.

The story of Rye lifeboats is complicated by the additional lifeboats at Camber on the other side of the river and the title Winchelsea used from 1862 to 1910 for Rye Harbour. While the ex-Dungeness boat was at Rye the Camber station was opened in 1857 with a new 28 foot × 6 foot, self-righter, built by Forrestt, pulling six oars and weighing 1 ton 5 cwt.

In 1861, the ex-Dungeness boat was replaced by a two ton boat originally built for Winterton, Norfolk, three years earlier. She was considerably larger, built by Forrestt to Peake's design, a 30 foot × 7 foot 7 inch boat, pulling ten oars and it is interesting to note that, by 1862, there were altogether 100 Peake boats in service all round the coasts. They had virtually become the standard self-righting lifeboat of the R.N.L.I. and were largely based on James Beeching's prize-winning design of 1851 modified and improved by James Peake. The main features of these boats were cork instead of air chambers along the bottom, both ends alike, steered by a steering oar and with a slightly raking stem and stern posts. They pulled either ten or twelve oars and were constructed of rock-elm, having side air-cases under the thwarts and raised ones at the ends up to gunwale height. These air-cases were of rubber between two layers of wood. Such a boat would clear herself of water in 55 seconds by draining tubes with automatic valves, and would right herself in seven seconds. With a seven cwt iron keel her total weight would be 2 tons 6 cwt and she could carry 30 people in addition to oarsmen, coxswain and bowman.

There were various alterations and amendments to the original design but the principal features remained the same and most of the boats were built by Forrestt of Limehouse.

It was this ex-Winterton boat that launched on service to the American ship *James Browne* in 1862 rescuing the crew of 18.

By 1866 the *Arthur Frederick*, a 37 foot × 7 foot 7 inch self-righter, built by Forrestt, was at Camber where she remained until 1881, being involved in a large number of services; among them to the Norwegian barque *Columbia* of Stavanger which ran ashore in fog and high wind nearly opposite the lifeboat house at about midnight on 7th April, 1869. She refloated at the next high tide and was escorted by the lifeboat to Dover.

A couple of years afterwards she was out in a heavy southerly gale to the brigantine *Cyrus* of Rye whose crew of nine were able to drop into the lifeboat as she veered in under the bowsprit. This was an exceptionally hazardous service, the lifeboat being right in the breakers throughout.

In October of the following year she was able to rescue the crew of two of the barge *Urgent* of Rochester which sank off Jury's Gap.

In her 27 launches on service the *Arthur Frederick* was able to rescue the fine total of 60 lives.

After saving 14 from the *Marie Amelie* of Quimper the Peake boat was replaced by the *Storm Sprite*, a 32 foot × 8 foot 2 inch self-righter, built by Forrestt, which was on station until 1883. Among her services was one to the brig *Elizabeth and Cicely* of Guernsey which went aground near the entrance to Rye Harbour. By skilful seamanship she was able to work in close and save the crew of eight who had taken to the rigging as the vessel began to break up in the pounding waves of a strong south-south-west gale. Altogether in her 16 years on the station 38 lives were saved.

Hastings lifeboat returning after rescuing crew of the F/V *Simon Peter*, 28th September, 1974. The lifeboat was the relief boat *Jane Hay*, a 37 foot Oakley, of similar pattern to the regular station boat *Fairlight*. 　　　　　　　　　　　*Photograph by Derek Cooper. R.N.L.I.*

The *Frances Harris*, ON 228, a 34 foot × 7 foot 9 inch self-righter took over duty from 1883 to 1899. She was built by Woolfe and again had the distinction of taking part in a big rescue of 18 men from the London barque *Warwickshire.*

At the same time Camber had the *Mary Stanford*, ON 236, a 34 foot × 7 foot 9 inch self-righter by Forrestt, which saved 35 lives before being replaced by the *Edward and Lucille*, ON 344, a 3 ton 16 cwt self-righter, built by Chambers and Colby of Lowestoft. She was, however, only launched twice in the course of her eight years on station and is not credited with the rescue of any lives.

By this time the decline in small coastal traders was making itself apparent, there was still a good fleet of trawlers working out of Rye Harbour but the larger vessels ploughing the channel were better found and with steam power already well advanced the likelihood of ships being in trouble in the Bay decreased. There seemed no longer any need for two stations on either side of the harbour mouth. In 1901 Camber was closed and the Rye Harbour boat took over the work.

John William Dudley, ON 453, was a 35 foot × 8 foot 6 inch self-righter built by Thames Ironworks, weighing 3 tons 16 cwt which came on station in 1900 serving right through till 1916. It is interesting to note the sudden escalation of costs, the *Frances Harris*, 1883, cost £363 whereas this new boat, seventeen years later, had increased to £831. Another interesting pointer to the change in the type of casualty was the large number of launches on service (42) compared with the number of lives saved (14). This did not mean that the services were in any way less arduous for the gallant fishermen who put out in her. Sometimes indeed they were of long duration, when, soaked by spray and numb with cold, the crew battled with mountainous seas for hours simply standing by a ship in danger. One such arduous job has already been mentioned in connection with Dungeness, the service to the *Lake Michigan* when the lifeboat crew was out for five days and nights.

There was another hazardous operation in May 1904 when in a strong south-westerly gale the ship *Derwent* of London broke adrift from her tug. There was an appalling smother of surf in Rye Bay when the alarm was given that a ship off Dengemarsh was flying signals for immediate assistance. The crew and shore helpers were assembled with all speed and the *John William Dudley* launched with some difficulty, the launchers having to wade in up to their necks to get the boat clear. At last she was away, found the *Derwent* and the lifeboat stood by until the weather eased sufficiently for the tow to be re-connected. Even then the spray-swept lifeboatmen had not finished their ordeal for the heavy seas that were running made it impossible for them to work back to their station. Instead they had to ride them all that night and did not reach Winchelsea until the next morning.

The tale of services went on, in June 1905, to the s.s. *Clara* of London in collision near to the Royal Sovereign Light Vessel. A tug took her in tow but by the time the lifeboat reached the spot her decks were awash and she was settling down. The lifeboat continued to stand by in case of need but finally the damaged vessel foundered off the Pett Coastguard Station and, when the crew had been transferred to the tug, the *John William Dudley* returned to base.

In 1909 it was a ketch, the *Lord Tennyson* of London and the crew of three together with their dog were rescued. Another smallish ship, in trouble off the harbour mouth, had been collecting grit from the beach to the west, but in a sudden strong wind she was blown on to the Camber sands and the two man crew had to be rescued by lifeboat.

With the coming of the First World War many of the hardy Rye fishermen served in the R.N.R. with distinction, but it was still possible to find a lifeboat crew. In 1916 the *Mary Stanford*, ON 661, came on station, a 38 foot × 10 foot 9 inch Liverpool type boat, built by Saunders of Cowes and weighing 4 tons 12 cwt. She was very similar to the Liverpool-type boat with which Henry Blogg carried out his famous service to the s.s. *Fernebo*. The number of launches on service during her twelve years was not very great and she had saved only ten lives when there occurred the tragic accident that, even today nearly fifty years later, is immediately associated with the Rye Harbour Station.

On 15th November, 1928, at about 6.30 a.m. in one of the worst gales Rye has known, news came through that the s.s. *Alice* of Riga was in distress. The sound of the maroons sent the volunteer lifeboat crew hurrying to the boat-house, launchers and helpers mustered but when they tried to launch the *Mary Stanford* she was flung back time and again. It was only when a number of the crew sprang over and helped that it proved possible to get her away. Within a few minutes news reached the Coastguard station that the *Alice's* crew had been taken off by another steamer so re-call signals were fired, but they were apparently, and quite understandably in such a storm, not heard. The *Mary Stanford* searched in vain for the distressed vessel and at about 10.30 a.m., having ridden out the worst of the gale, was sighted by a passing vessel, putting back towards Rye Harbour. Frequently when out in really severe weather the Rye lifeboat would make for Folkestone or else lie offshore, but on this occasion she returned towards the harbour under sail. In the terrible following seas off the harbour entrance she capsized and every member of the 17 man crew lost his life.

At nearly every lifeboat station in the country there is a strong family connection; and here at Rye the tragedy struck at the whole fishing community. Herbert Head, the coxswain had his two sons James and John with him, J. Stonham was second coxswain and H. Cutting, the bowman, was with his brothers Robert and Albert, Charles, Robert and Alexander Pope were three brothers, William and Leslie Clark were brothers, Maurice and Arthur Downey were cousins and the remaining crew were H. Smith, W. Igglesden and C. Southerden.

The whole country was shocked and saddened by the disaster, the worst that had befallen the lifeboat service for many years, and a local fund for the dependents realised over £35,000. A memorial tablet of Manx stone was presented to Rye Harbour by the people of the Isle of Man; and a memorial stained glass window was placed in Winchelsea Church. A fitting tribute to the courage and self-sacrifice of these volunteers was paid by H.R.H. Edward, Prince of Wales* at a R.N.L.I. meeting in the Usher Hall, Edinburgh, the following year when he said,

*President of the R.N.L.I. from 1919 to 1936.

"the Rye Lifeboat crew had carried on the traditions of a service which, like every fighting service, had always involved the risk of the supreme sacrifice. Such men gave their lives for the common weal, and in so doing, won for themselves the praise that grows not old. Such tragedies were an inseparable part of the great enduring drama of the sea, and lent to the lives and death of the lifeboatmen an element of the sublime."

The station was closed in 1928 and for many years the old boat-house and the local memorial statue of the lifeboatman fully clad in oilskins and life-jacket, with a coil of rope in his hand were mute reminders of the 231 lives saved by the Rye lifeboats and the three gold and six silver medals awarded for outstanding skill and gallantry. In recent years, with the establishment of a holiday camp at Camber and the great upsurge of visitors and small-boat sailors, the R.N.L.I. decided to place an Inshore Lifeboat at Rye Harbour. Once again a dedicated band of volunteers stand ready throughout the summer months to launch to the rescue. In the first eight years on station in 110 launches, they have rescued 34. Among the crew were three brothers, Ron, Teddy and Dave Caister, Keith Downey, whose uncle was drowned in the *Mary Stanford* disaster and Terry Broockes had his son Kevin in the crew.

Westward of Fairlight is the premier town of the Cinque Ports, Hastings, with its historic origins going right back to Saxon times, but its greatest development and expansion dates from the end of the eighteenth century, like Margate and other seaside towns, as a result of sea-bathing coming into fashion. But, at Hastings, unlike so many of the Cinque Ports, the great tidal flow of the Channel eroded the cliffs, and instead of the town being left inland like New Romney, Sandwich, Rye or Winchelsea with only a tenuous connection with the sea, it is still a prominent seaside resort although the original harbour had ceased to be of much account by Elizabethan times. Like all the Cinque Ports it suffered much at the hands of the French in 1359 and 1377 and, according to R. F. Jessup,* "by the middle of the 16th century it was described as being reduced to 'waste, destruction and poverty'".

Through the ages the sailors of Hastings have been well known. They sent five ships to the siege of Calais in 1347, there were Hastings men in the running fight against the Spanish Armada, the fishing fleet has been of importance to the town ever since the Cinque Ports were granted the privilege of "den and strond", the right to land and dry their fishing nets at Yarmouth, far to the north in East Anglia. Fish from here were sent to London by packhorse during the Stuart times and even today the fishing boats are drawn up on the shingle near The Stade, and the lifeboat crew, as has been the case since 1858, is mainly comprised of fishermen.

At twenty past eight on the morning of 28th September, 1974 word came through from the Fairlight Coastguard that a fishing vessel was in distress some two and a half miles to the south west of Rye Harbour. There was a gale force south-westerly wind with waves of 15 to 20 feet breaking on the beach and the reserve lifeboat, *Jane Hay*, a 37 foot Oakley, was on station. The maroons were fired

The Cinque Ports. Batsford, 1952.

and preparations made to launch in what the official report described as "the worst conditions in which a carriage launch has ever been attempted at this station". Coxswain Joe Martin had to use all his skill and judgement in assessing the right moment to minimise the risk of hitting the sand and being knocked back on to the carriage by the next wave, or being broached while the boat was still on the carriage. The right moment came and, with outstanding teamwork and judgement, the boat was got away.

The wind was still increasing as the coxswain began his search for the casualty. The Coastguard helicopter and the Dungeness lifeboat were also on duty but the clouds were scudding very low and for some time the search proved fruitless. Shortly before 11 a.m. radio contact was again made with the casualty, the *Simon Peter*, and as a result the helicopter located her some three and a half miles from Hastings harbour and the *Jane Hay* headed in that direction. A R.A.F. helicopter now took over, when the original helicopter had to return to base to refuel, and she directed the lifeboat to the distressed vessel.

The fishing boat was in a desperate position with waves 30 to 40 feet in height breaking over her, wrecking her wheel-house. Heading in towards her the coxswain directed the men to let go their anchor and prepare to be taken off. When this had been done he made his first run in alongside, heading into the wind and the tremendous seas. He found the *Simon Peter's* crew too exhausted to do anything to help themselves so he put his engines astern and dropped back instructing his men to board if necessary and fetch them. Then, judging the run of the tide and the effect of the seas with consummate skill he made his second approach. Second Coxswain White leant across between the two wildly heaving boats and secured the head rope and all the while ignoring the great risk that he might be crushed between them. In seconds two of the exhausted men were dragged across to safety followed by the skipper, the second coxswain cut the rope and Coxswain Martin put his engines full astern, to avoid the lifeboat carrying right on to the casualty.

The whole of this action had taken place in terrible conditions and was a superb example of skill when the slightest error might well have been disastrous or at the very least have damaged the lifeboat severely.

It was clearly essential to get the shipwrecked men ashore with the utmost speed so, in spite of it being an hour and a half before low water, the coxswain let out his drogue to check the *Jane Hay* in the heavy following seas, crossed the bar and drove straight for the beach bumping over the sandy bottom as he went. Ashore, in the howling wind and rain, a crowd of enthusiastic helpers had gathered under head launcher Ronald White and they quickly and efficiently hauled the boat clear of the breakers.

For this very gallant service the silver medal was awarded to Coxswain Joe Martin, the Second Coxswain George Douglas White received the bronze medal for his courageous work in securing the boats, while the Thanks of the Institution inscribed on vellum were awarded to Assistant Mechanic Harry Benson, Second Assistant Robert Shoesmith and crew members Richard Adams, Michael Barrow,

Launching the Hastings lifeboat. Note the steep shingle beach and fishing boats drawn up in the background. *Photograph by Barratt Photo Press.   R.N.L.I.*

Albert White and Richard Read. A framed letter of thanks was also awarded to the head launcher Ronald White. Coxswain Kirkaldie often put the question when his lifeboat *Prudential* was away for overhaul, "Why do emergencies so often happen when reserve boats are on station?". His counterpart, Joe Martin, possibly thought along the same lines but probably when he took the *Jane Hay* to sea on this occasion the launch most occupied his mind. Beach launches, particularly from shingle, have always provided awkward problems not only at Hastings but at other stations where no other feasible launching method is possible or available. Coxswain Martin's views sum up the main problem very well; he considers the first 100 yards are always the most critical and similarly the last 100 yards coming back. Anyone who has tried to launch any boat through the breakers of even the mildest sea will understand the problem.

Imagine how difficult it must have been when horses were used to drag the launching carriage. Even when the first motor lifeboat came here horses were still being used and Joe Martin, as a young boy, often watched them hauling the carriage. His is one of the many lifeboat families of Hastings, his father having served in the boat for forty years and Adams and White are other names that are inseparable from the Hastings boat. All these gallant volunteers feel the same as Coxswain Derek Scott of the Mumbles, who said in his speech at the 1974 Annual General Meeting, in celebration of the 150th anniversary of the Service, "if you could . . . share with me and see the look on a survivor's face at the moment of rescue and share that marvellous feeling with the lifeboatmen when they are coming home in the boat and the job has been done, then you would all know that this last 150 years has been more than worthwhile."

Some time before 1850 the local fishermen had a rescue boat at Hastings but details of her or of her services are not known. All we do know is that no seaman would ever see lives lost in a shipwreck if he could manage to put out to the rescue. True to this spirit Lieutenants John Prattent, R.N. and Horatio James, R.N. saved nine of the crew of a French lugger *La Constance*, for which the R.N.L.I. awarded them gold medals. About 1850 this early boat was reported to be "out of repair" and eight years later the local inhabitants, shocked by a wreck in which all the crew perished, requested the R.N.L.I. to establish a station.

The lifeboat *Victoria* was therefore placed on station, a 30 foot 4 inch × 8 foot 2 inch self-righter built by Forrestt, and she was followed in 1865 by an unnamed boat which had been built in 1854 and then lengthened to 36 foot 4 inch × 8 foot 2 inch. Her cost was originally £197 whilst the present day station boat *Fairlight*, built 110 years later, cost £33,000. This unnamed boat was presently christened *Ellen Goodman* and served here until 1880 only having three service launches in all that time and saving five lives.

The *Charles Arkcoll*, ON 187, followed in 1880, and she was a self-righter of 34 foot × 8 foot 8 inches built by Woolfe. Again the number of launches was small, but with the second *Charles Arkcoll*, ON 469, 35 foot × 8 foot 6 inch pulling ten oars the services increased. It was during this boat's long spell of duty from 1901-31 that John (Joe) Martin's father joined the crew, at a time when the great shire horses would plunge and heave at the launching carriage to drag the boat down to the water on her missions of mercy. The carriage had 12 inch tyres and was fitted with horse launching poles on either side.

As at all lifeboat stations a wide variety of services was undertaken. One type of service was to assist a vessel on fire, some of the crew going aboard to help with the fire-fighting while the lifeboat stood by to take off the men if the flames got out of hand and an example of this happened in April 1906 on service to the s.s. *Lugano* of Hamburg. Another was to help steamers whose engines had broken down, as was the case of the *Volano* of Sunderland, when the lifeboat battled with a very heavy sea to fetch a tug to assist and then returned with her to the vessel.

April 1908 was a stormy month and on the evening of the 25th the *Charles Arkcoll* launched at 6.20 p.m. on what was to be a most arduous and lengthy service in bitter conditions. There was a west-south-westerly gale blowing at the time with blinding snow making the problems of launching even more involved. The difficulties of launching-horses under these circumstances may be imagined when combined with heavy surf pounding the beach. The barge *Amy* of London which had been riding at anchor off St Leonard's after losing both her topmast and bowsprit, had gone adrift after her anchor cable parted and now she was in grave danger of piling up on the shore.

Fortunately, the wind began to veer and by the time the lifeboat reached her, she was managing to claw off the beach. Running alongside the lifeboatmen boarded the barge, the captain asking them to help him to a safe anchorage as he and his crew were utterly exhausted. With the lifeboat coxswain and his men taking turns at the wheel, they steered the barge round into Dungeness East Bay. The weather was too bad for the lifeboat to beat back to Hastings so instead she was beached at Dungeness at 2 a.m., the crew returning home by train. Later the following day when the weather had moderated she was brought back to her station.

A very special occasion at Hastings was in 1927 when Edward Prince of Wales (later Edward VIII) visited the town to open the White Rock Pavilion and the New Promenade. As President of the R.N.L.I. he had earlier presided over the Annual General Meeting in 1921 and announced the formation of the Ladies' Lifeboat Guild. This organisation, whose members have contributed such tireless enthusiasm and devotion to the lifeboat cause in so many districts, has been foremost in fund-raising campaigns. Now he went on board the Hastings lifeboat where Coxswain J. Plummer and the members of the crew were presented to him. While there he was made a member of the famous Winkle Club and presented with a gold winkle by the oldest working fisherman.

After a notable period on service and rescuing 28 lives, the *Charles Arkcoll* was replaced by the *Cyril and Lilian Bishop*, ON 740, one of the boats presented to Sussex stations by Mrs L. Philpott; the other being at Newhaven. She was a motor-driven self-righting lifeboat of 35½ foot × 8 foot 10 inch, built by J. Samuel White of Cowes and was one of the R.N.L.I. boats to see service at Dunkirk. A local report describes the large crowds that gathered on the beach at the Fishmarket to welcome the new boat on her arrival from Cowes. "The weather was hazy in the distance so the lifeboat was not sighted until she was near home but the beach was black with people long before she arrived." Coxswain W. Curtis told a reporter of the local newspaper, "We had a pleasant trip. We thoroughly enjoyed it. The *Cyril and Lilian Bishop* is a fine craft and a smart one—every inch a boat. She handles very well and is quick on the helm." With him on the journey from Cowes he had motor mechanic W. Hilder, Frank Martin the bowman, and Fred Doughty.

As the *Cyril and Lilian Bishop* weighed 6 tons 2 cwt compared with the 3 tons 16 cwt of the *Charles Arkcoll* special caterpillar wheels were fitted to the old carriage to support the increased weight on the loose shingle, but the old method of using horses to draw the carriage still remained for a short while. One of her first launches was in 1931 on the occasion of the South Eastern Conference at the White Rock Pavilion when delegates from south east branches were taken on a short trip to Dungeness.

What a contrast between this peaceful scene and the splendid service twelve years later when seven men were saved from H.M. Trawler *Gaulonia* which had been wrecked south of Jury's Gap. Heavy seas were breaking over her but Coxswain John Muggeridge held the lifeboat alongside for half an hour until all seven men were safely taken off. Both Coxswain Muggeridge and Mechanic W. Hilder were awarded the bronze medal for gallantry on this service while the Institution's thanks on vellum were awarded to Commander Highfield, the Honorary Secretary, Second Coxswain E. F. Adams and Bowman I. F. P. White. But a few days after he won this medal Coxswain Muggeridge was killed when his fishing boat struck a mine, and eight weeks later motor mechanic Hilder lost his life in an air-raid.

The following year provided yet another warning of the perils faced by the volunteers of the lifeboat service for while she was out searching for a landing craft in very rough seas the lifeboat capsized, the coxswain and two members of the crew being washed out of her although mercifully they were rescued.

Finally after 99 launches in which 34 lives were saved the *Cyril and Lilian Bishop* was replaced in 1950 by the *MTC*, ON 878, the gift of the Trained Women Driver's Club. This boat was built by Groves and Guttridge of East Cowes and was again a self-righter of 35½ foot × 10 foot, costing over £11,000 and the tally of service launches increased, although the number of lives saved was relatively small.

Frequently she went out to escort ships that had been damaged in collision. She joined the Dungeness lifeboat on the night of 1st January, 1959 after a very difficult launch in a west-south-westerly gale when the tide was low, locating and escorting the house-boat *Petrina* which was taken in tow by Dungeness.

Next time these two lifeboats were out on service together it was the Hastings boat that towed the local fishing-boat *Breadwinner* and Dungeness stood by. As with all the other stations round the coast, more and more of the services were to yachts — in distress through engine failure, ignorance or gear coming adrift. One of these incidents, when five people might have been in serious trouble, was in July 1959. The sea was moderate but, with a strong west-south-west wind, it was getting rougher. Just before 9 p.m. on the 11th the Coastguard reported a yacht in difficulties nine miles south east by south. When *MTC* drew near she found the yacht *Panda* with the cross-trees unshipped so that she could not set any canvas. The *MTC* took her in tow to Rye Harbour which was reached at 2.07 a.m., and after the *Panda* was moored safely the lifeboat returned to her station at 5.14 a.m. There were also services to local fishing boats, for example the *Valiant*, in December 1959. With engine failure she was in a dangerous position near rocks and within 50 yards of the eastern groyne. Other boats tried to take her in tow but with the help of the lifeboat she was brought as close to shore as possible and then warped ashore by hand.

On the morning of 1st July, 1961 the Coastguard reported an explosion and a fire two and a half miles off Fairlight. The *MTC* launched in smooth conditions to find the yacht *Lady Alice* entirely shattered by an explosion. Making a search of the area the lifeboat found the sole occupant clinging to an upturned dinghy so he was hauled aboard and efforts were made to tow the wreck ashore but she very soon sank. The survivor was given food and clothing by the second coxswain's brother and later taken back to Rye Harbour. Again in August she was called to a yacht, the *Aimée-Léone*, which was firing red flares. In the fresh west-south-west wind the crew of five were seasick and exhausted, the skipper declaring he could not sail any further so, with lifeboatmen aboard to take charge, a long and tricky tow began to Newhaven.

With so many incidents involving small craft it was decided to add an Inshore Lifeboat to the station in 1964. That year also saw the *MTC*, after 107 launches, replaced by the present lifeboat *Fairlight*, ON 973, a 37 foot × 11½ foot Oakley, built by William Osborne of Littlehampton. It was in the I.L.B. that Joe Martin won a framed letter of thanks from the R.N.L.I. as did Police Sergeant S. Ferguson who helped him man the boat to rescue a drowning man. In 1967 Joe Martin and W. Adams manned the I.L.B. to rescue four people from two capsized sailing boats winning further letters of thanks.

In 1965 there were further services to yachts in trouble, to local fishing vessels and a coaster with engine failure. The list of services increased year by year until in 1972 there occurred an extraordinary incident when the crew of the I.L.B. were awarded framed letters of thanks for their seamanship and judgement when assisting a badly injured man who had fallen over the cliff at Ecclesbourne Glen. The Honorary Secretary Mr J. J. Adams felt grave doubts about launching the I.L.B. with such a short steep sea on the beach but the police requested assistance so at 2.37 p.m. helmsman R. Shoesmith, C. Green and K. Ronchetti launched. Making all speed in the existing conditions they beached near the casualty at 3.05 p.m., only able to do so in such a rocky treacherous spot by superb seamanship and local knowledge. Seeing the injured man's condition and suspecting a fractured skull the helmsman considered it unwise to risk him in the I.L.B. so, as the Fairlight Cliff Rescue team was now at hand, he was very carefully hoisted to the top. By now the weather was much worse with a very dangerous sea pounding the beach; so it was decided to try to recover the I.L.B. up the cliff face. While the exhausted crew were driven back to Hastings, Joe Martin now took charge assisted by lifeboatman B. Foster, head launcher Ronald White and the Cliff Rescue team under Coastguard F. Davis. In driving rain they managed to hoist her up successfully, and a farmer, Mr Usher, then towed the I.L.B. in a trailer back to station.

It is not always only the lifeboat crew who face danger in volunteering to save life at sea. On 23rd December, 1974 the Fairlight Coastguard gave information that there had been an explosion aboard an Argentinian warship the *Candido de Lasala* and the services of a doctor were needed. Maroons were fired and the reserve lifeboat *Jane Hay* launched in a moderate sea with a fresh south by east breeze with Dr Peter Davy, the Honorary Medical Officer, on board.

They had travelled about one and a half miles in the direction of the warship when a rescue helicopter made contact and Dr Davy was asked to transfer to the aircraft so that he could reach the injured man more quickly. The lifeboat crew were briefed, speed was increased and the helicopter hovered overhead while the second crewman was lowered to the *Jane Hay*. After several efforts he landed on board but whilst he was putting Dr Davy into the second strap the helicopter lost contact. The two men were dragged off the lifeboat, the rope swinging to and fro like a pendulum, and they were dashed against the stern of the lifeboat before being separated in the water. When the helicopter was back in position Dr Davy was picked up and then taken to the warship where he was able to treat the injured men. One of them had to be transferred to hospital by helicopter, together with the doctor. Only when he had made sure that his patient was being properly cared for did Dr Davy allow himself to be examined and it was discovered that he had tended the injured whilst he himself had seven broken ribs and must have been in very great pain. The silver medal for gallantry was awarded to Dr Davy by the R.N.L.I.

This award brings the record of medals for Hastings station to two gold, two silver and three bronze in the course of the large total of 361 service launches, in which 185 lives have been saved.

Naming ceremony of new lifeboat *Fairlight* in 1964. *Photograph by George E. Gregory* *R.N.L.I.*

CHAPTER SEVEN

BEACHY HEAD

Eastbourne

THE 90 mile coast-line of Sussex is unique in its array of large and spacious seaside towns, each one with its own peculiar charm, and the various alterations in the nature of the cliffs, some sandstone, others mighty cliffs of chalk, like Beachy Head where the South Downs culminate. The marshy land of Pevensey, which was once attached to the Cinque Port of Hastings and earlier still was one of the great Roman forts used by the Classis Britannica, the British fleet, leads back to the area once clothed in dense forests of oak. Here the South Saxons invaded and according to the *Anglo Saxon Chronicle* slew all the men in the camp. The Vikings used this harbour and William of Normandy landed here but gradually the little streams of the Pevensey level silted up the harbour until, by the nineteenth century, only small ships could make any use of the haven. Westward however the land began to rise to the contours of the Downs. Here there grew up the third largest town of Sussex, Eastbourne, which is the latest of the great seaside resorts. Right up to the middle of the nineteenth century there was only the Old Town and two small hamlets, Meads and Southborne, together with a cluster of buildings, known as Sea Houses, on the shore. Then the development, orderly and spacious, began and culminated in what is today the three miles of pleasingly laid out front. The beach is shingle with sand further sea-ward, at about the half tide level, so when it was decided to place a lifeboat here, it had to be of such a size and design that it could be conveniently launched from the beach. What made the stationing of a lifeboat here more important was the ever present danger of ships running on to Beachy Head in thick weather, as many had done in earlier years, before the building of a lighthouse. The first light was the Belle Tout about a mile westward of the actual top of the headland, erected in 1831. Parson Darby's hole, cut in the cliff-face, was supposedly to provide shelter for shipwrecked sailors, being a way through to the top of the Head. It is possible, though, that this was used for the running of illicit cargoes. Certainly many such cargoes found their way through Birling Gap a short way further westward.

Mr John Fuller, M.P., of Rose Hill, provided the first boat in 1822 but exactly whereabouts it was kept is uncertain. She was of local design, 25 feet × 8 feet 6 inches and was built by Simpson, a local builder. She pulled ten oars, was given additional buoyancy by means of casks lashed between and beneath the thwarts but was not self-righting. She did, however, have special tubes to assist her to free herself of water.

When Mr Fuller died in 1833 he left his boat "to the inhabitants of Eastbourne" and she continued on station till 1863. She was still in operation when

Incidents like this were the reason for the establishment of Eastbourne lifeboat. *Emma Louise* aground at Beachy Head.   *A. S. Payne*

the local lifeboat committee asked the R.N.L.I. to take over responsibility for the running of the station in 1853.

True to the traditions of British seamen to lend assistance to those in distress there had already been a very gallant service in 1824 when Lieutenant Joseph Clarke helped to save the crew of five and the pilot from the *June* ashore at Birling Gap. The R.N.L.I. presented him with the gold medal for his gallant action which was undertaken in a furious storm.

Another early service was in 1833 when the ship *Isabella* was wrecked during a hurricane and broke up. The local fishermen launched off in the lifeboat and, double-banking the oars, managed to rescue the 29 people aboard, in two trips.

The silver medal for gallantry was awarded during this time to Lieutenant Blair of the Coastguards for rescuing four from a French lugger and also to Lieutenant Gilson R.N. for rescuing four from a French schooner off Beachy Head.

There was an unusual award in 1845 by the South Holland Society for Saving the Shipwrecked which presented a silver medal and a diploma to all the lifeboat crew for their rescue of the master and nine seamen from the Dutch East Indiaman *Twee Cornelissen* which had driven ashore in a storm in Pevensey Bay. With great skill and seamanship the lifeboatmen managed to veer alongside the rigging and take off the survivors, whilst other members of the crew contrived to get ashore in the ship's boat. The coxswain at this time was Samuel Knight who was succeeded in 1853 by Joseph Huggett who held the post for the next twenty-seven years; and here again, as in so many of our lifeboat stations, comes a great family link with the boat, Derek Huggett being the present coxswain. Another family, the Allchorns, has an equally fine record of service in the boat, Thomas Allchorn being a member of the crew at the service to the Dutch vessel mentioned above and his brother Edward was in the crew which launched to the *Isabella*.

In 1863 it was decided to station a new lifeboat at Eastbourne and the site chosen for her station was near the Wish Tower, a Martello tower at the west of the front. This boat was the *Mary Stirling*, a 33 foot × 8 foot 10 inch self-righter, built by Forrestt which was on station for the next seventeen years. During this time she launched on service only five times. The next boat, the *William and Mary*, ON 186, a 34 foot × 8½ foot self-righter had twelve services during her 19 years on station but an unfortunate accident marred her arrival. When she was being drawn through the streets on her carriage a small boy, Ernest Best, was so eager to see the detail of the new boat that he allowed one of the wheels to run over his foot. It was so severely injured that it had to be amputated but the donors of the new boat in Manchester undertook to pay all the medical expenses and the R.N.L.I. made a special grant to him.

1883 was a momentous year for this boat. On 24th September word was received from the Coastguards at Bexhill that a Norwegian barque, the *Isabella*, was ashore. In a severe south-westerly gale the *William and Mary* launched and on reaching the scene found the vessel being pounded heavily by monstrous seas. Her foremast had gone by the board,* and veering down on her anchor cable the lifeboat was able to work under the stern from which the eight crew were rescued.

On 25th November of the same year there occurred one of the most famous of the Eastbourne rescues. News came that the Norwegian barque *New Brunswick* was flying signals of distress off Belle Tout Lighthouse. There was a furious south-south-westerly gale and it was obvious that, even if she was able to launch, it would be impossible for the *William and Mary* to work round Beachy Head in the teeth of the gale. A crowd of willing helpers together with a team of horses set about the daunting task of dragging the boat on her carriage right over the Downs to Birling Gap from which she would be able to launch with the wind and seas more in her favour. They had to drag her for five miles, climbing in all 600 feet and even though extra horses joined the team on the way, it was hard going. When they reached the gap the lifeboatmen found that the gap was too narrow for the carriage so the boat was dragged down, sections of the bank were cut away to let her pass through the narrow way, and skids improvised to help her launch. At length the lifeboat got away and, labouring at the oars in the furious sea, the heroic crew managed to work in close enough to the casualty for a rope to be thrown and the eleven men aboard were saved.

As this service had been carried out with such splendid determination and no difficulty had deterred the lifeboatmen in their mission of mercy the R.N.L.I. doubled the normal awards and additional sums were raised by local collections (some £70) and by the donor of the boat (£20). Unhappily a claim for life salvage was made against the Norwegian owners, an action absolutely contrary to the

---

*By the board is a nautical term and in this case indicates it has either been broken off close to the deck or gone over the side — overboard.

regulations of the R.N.L.I. Although warned by the Institution that such an act was in direct contravention of the rules the lifeboatmen still continued with their claim and were paid £120. With the concurrence of the local committee, the coxswain and crew were dismissed. The boat and boat-house were put in charge of a boat-house keeper who was to authorise its use to any reputable body of seamen or reputable persons in the event of a wreck.

This very unhappy sequel to a fine rescue was necessary to clarify the position of the Institution and maintain its good name. If once the impression was given that crews were interested in money rather than in saving life, the whole concept of the R.N.L.I. would be spoiled for the great majority of crews who obeyed the spirit and letter of the rules and fully approved of them.

A new crew under Coxswain Jesse Huggett in 1887, carried out another dangerous service in driving snow when they rescued the 16 men aboard the Norwegian barque *Sjodroninjan* wrecked near the Belle Tout Lighthouse.

The list of services continued including standing by the *Normandy* bound for Dieppe from Newhaven, in company with the Newhaven lifeboat *Michael Henry*; landing an injured seaman from the Royal Sovereign Lightship; rescuing four men and a boy from the Hasting's lugger *Bantham* and going to the aid of the steam yacht *Ray* of Dover.

In 1890 new methods for summoning the crews were decided upon, a bell mounted on the coxswain's house, but that did not always prove sufficiently audible so in 1903 a mortar was supplied to the No 1 station—by this time there were two lifeboats, No 1 at the Wish Tower and No 2 at the fishing boat beach at the eastern end of the town.

Eastbourne lifeboat *James Stevens No. 6* (ON 427). On service 1899-1924, then on exhibition till 1935.
From an old postcard

The William Terriss boat-house at Eastbourne, now the Lifeboat Museum.

Photograph by Larkin Bros.   R.N.L.I.

In 1899 a new boat, built by Roberts of Mevagissey, the *James Stevens No 6*, ON 427, was sent to the No 1 station in place of the *William and Mary* which had saved 45 lives in her 19 years. The new boat was a self-righter pulling ten oars, 35 foot × 8½ foot, and was on service until 1924. She was housed in a new specially built boat-house the funds for which were raised by the *Daily Telegraph* in memory of the famous actor William Terriss. This boat-house is now the Eastbourne Lifeboat Museum, the first permanent lifeboat museum to be established in Britain and opened as such in 1937.

It was in this boat that there occurred one of those accidents which serve as a reminder of the eternal strength and danger of the sea, danger that is always at the elbow of those who go afloat. In a service to the s.s. *Southport* in monstrous seas on 8th November, 1902, two lifeboatmen were washed out of the boat. Fortunately their lifejackets kept them afloat and they were soon recovered.

It was in 1902 that the No 2 station was established at the fishing beach, a new boat-house being built there to take a 36 foot × 9 foot, Liverpool type boat, pulling twelve oars and built by Thames Ironworks. This boat, the *Olive*, was on station until 1919 but only five launches were recorded in all that time, most of them to stand by vessels in difficulty.

The *James Stevens No 6* meanwhile was on call many times. In fact her number of service launches (43) was the highest until the days of the modern motor lifeboats. During this time Ben Erridge was coxswain till 1911. On one occasion, in

November, 1904, the fishing fleet was caught by a sudden south-westerly gale off Pevensey. Ben Erridge himself and the second coxswain were afloat but they managed to reach the shore and bring out the lifeboat. Already one fishing boat had gone ashore and had become a total wreck. The *James Stevens* stood by the remaining five until they were beached safely. It was reported that the lifeboat had behaved splendidly in very rough seas.

On 18th March, 1906, a very wet cold day, a vessel was reported ashore on a reef off Beachy Head at 7.30 a.m. The *James Stevens* was quickly on the scene, picking up four of the crew in the ship's boat on the way. Then the lifeboatmen stood by in case of need while every effort was made to save the schooner which was the *Laura Williamson* of Boston. Presently the crew, fearing that the mast would go by the board, asked to be taken off. Later further attempts to refloat the vessel by the lifeboatmen, the crew and a tug were successful and she was pulled clear and towed to Newhaven escorted by the lifeboat. The *James Stevens* finally returned to her station at midnight, the crew exhausted after a heavy day's work.

One of the most unusual services carried out during these years was when the P & O outward bound liner *Oceana* was involved in a collision with the German barque *Pisagua* off Beachy Head. It was just after 4 a.m. on a windy March morning in 1912. The heavily laden *Pisagua*, a four-master of nearly 3,000 tons belonging to the famous Laeisz line, was beating up-channel under full press of sail and the liner failed to give her right of way. In the resultant collision the liner was holed so badly that she sank. *James Stevens No 6* under Coxswain Erridge launched and picked up 21 survivors from a ship's boat. Taking them ashore she then put out again, being joined by the Newhaven boat, and together they were able to transfer the remaining passengers to the cross-channel steamer *Sussex*. The two lifeboats

London steamer *Barnhill* on fire off Beachy Head, 20th March, 1940, after attack by German aircraft. Lifeboat *Jane Holland* standing by. Two of her crew, Thomas Allchorn and Alec Huggett, boarded the blazing ship to rescue the unconscious captain.

Photograph by H. C. Deal of Eastbourne.   R.N.L.I.

then continued to stand by until the *Oceana* sunk, *James Stevens No 6* returning to her station after six hours at sea. The *Pisagua* also was severely damaged and did not sail for Laeisz again.

During the First World War under Coxswain Harry Erridge *James Stevens No 6* was much engaged in rescuing survivors from ships sunk by mines or torpedoes.

By 1924 it had been decided to withdraw the *James Stevens No 6* after her fine record of 34 lives saved but she continued her duties as an exhibition lifeboat in the William Terriss Memorial Boat-house. Thousands of people had the chance of viewing her there before she was finally removed in 1935 and sold to Allchorn Bros who had been running pleasure boats from Eastbourne beach since 1861. They converted her by fitting a 30 h.p. Atlantic engine and she was in use until the Second World War when she went across to Dunkirk. Her carriage was altered into a mobile landing stage for pleasure-boat passengers and this was still in use for this purpose until recently.

Steps were taken to send a motor lifeboat to Eastbourne on trial, with a view to assessing the possibilities of launching such a boat from a carriage. This was the *Priscilla Macbean*, ON 655, a 35 foot × 8½ foot self-righter, built by J. Samuel White of Cowes, powered by a 15 h.p. Miller engine and she took the place of the *Olive*, on service here until 1927, being launched 11 times and saving six lives. She was then moved to Kirkcudbright till 1931 and was afterwards at Maryport till 1934, finally becoming a private yacht.

After the experience gained with the prototype motor self-righter a second boat of this class came to Eastbourne in 1927, the *L.P and St Helens*, ON 703. She was 35 foot × 8 foot 10 inch, built by Saunders of Cowes and her weight 4 tons 15 cwt. She had a more powerful engine, a 34 h.p. Weyburn which gave her a speed of something in the region of 7 knots, and after only two years she was transferred to Boulmer in Northumberland.

After testing the capabilities of these two light motor lifeboats the larger *Jane Holland*, ON 673, came here from Selsey. She had been built by J. Samuel White of Cowes in 1922, was a 40 foot × 10½ foot self-righting motor lifeboat and had already saved 11 lives. She was to be the Eastbourne lifeboat for twenty years, during which time she saw gallant service throughout the Second World War and also was one of the 19 R.N.L.I. boats at Dunkirk. Under Coxswain Michael Hardy she was launched on service no less than 55 times, rescuing 65 lives, 42 of these during the war. One of her greatest services was to the steamer *Barnhill* of London which was attacked by German aircraft on 20th March, 1940. In the course of this service two of the lifeboat crew, Thomas Allchorn and Alec Huggett, volunteered to go aboard the fiercely burning ship to search for an injured man. He turned out to be the captain of the ship and unconscious when they found him. Coxswain Hardy brought the *Jane Holland* alongside and the injured man was safely transferred. For their very gallant action the R.N.L.I. awarded the bronze medal for gallantry to Thomas Allchorn and Alec Huggett and a formal letter of thanks to Coxswain Michael Hardy for his skilful and courageous handling of the boat.

The *Jane Holland's* post-war services were principally to motor-boats or small sailing craft and in 1949 she was replaced by the present lifeboat, *Beryl Tollemache*, ON 859.* *Jane Holland* went into the reserve fleet for four years, then was sold to a Southampton firm who re-named her *Reporter*.

The *Beryl Tollemache* is a 41 foot × 12 foot 3 inch Beach type motor lifeboat, weighing about 15 tons and built by the Sussex Yacht Co of Shoreham at a cost of £15,000. She is the first of the Beach type to be equipped with a cabin and was built as a result of a gift by Sir Lyonel and Lady Tollemache in memory of their daughter. This gift not only provides for the present lifeboat but for the subsequent lifeboats at Eastbourne which will also bear the same name.

At the naming ceremony in July 1949 Sir Godfrey Baring, Chairman of the Committee of Management of the R.N.L.I. said "I am quite certain of this, that when the maroon is fired as a signal of distress, that there is a casualty to be attended to, the Eastbourne lifeboatmen, in the performance of their noble and gallant duty, will display the noblest characteristics of our race — courage, persistence and self-sacrifice".

It was only six years later that, after a number of relatively minor services, the crew of the *Beryl Tollemache* showed just these qualities.

During a dense fog on the 26th April, 1955 the Greek steamer *Germania* of the Piraeus was in collision with a Panamanian steamer the *Maro* out in the channel about four miles off Beachy Head. Her captain decided to work in-shore and anchor where the extent of the damage could be discovered but unfortunately his vessel ran aground a short distance east of Beachy Head Lighthouse. At once the maroons were fired and Coxswain Thomas Allchorn and his crew launched the *Beryl Tollemache* at 4.45 p.m. As they approached the steamer the coxswain had great difficulty in picking his way through a maze of rocks to reach her; but he succeeded in taking off the crew of 26. The captain, his chief officer and one of the seamen then decided to return on board so the other 23 were landed and the lifeboat returned to stand by throughout the night.

Despite the fear that the *Germania* had broken her back a number of salvage boats were busily employed on the wreck for the following ten days but by the 6th May the weather had turned dirty, with a strong south-westerly gale and a rough sea. In late afternoon flares were seen from the wreck and the *Beryl Tollemache* was launched. On her way out to the wreck she came up with the *Endeavour*, one of the salvage boats, and took her crew of two on board but, while towing this boat, they had a radio message from another salvage boat, the *Moonbeam*. This boat was also taken in tow with some difficulty and at length they were brought safely back to the vicinity of the pier and anchored there. While the lifeboatmen were still struggling to bring the *Endeavour* and the *Moonbeam* to safety they heard yet another radio message reporting flares from the *Germania* so Coxswain Allchorn set out once more for the wreck, reaching her at half-past nine. By this time the sea was heavy and there was a full south-westerly gale. It was also pitch dark so the approach among the rocks was doubly dangerous. Great spouts of white foam could

---

*Beryl Tollemache is now in reserve with *Charles Dibdin, Civil Service No 32* as station boat until a new 37 foot Rother class comes into service in 1978. She will be called *Duke of Kent* in honour of the Silver Jubilee.

Coxswain Tom Allchorn at the wheel.
Photograph by Eastbourne Gazette.   R.N.L.I.

be seen as the breakers thundered against the wreck, broken water dashing as high as the masts and funnel. Clearly it would be impossible to approach the port side; but to starboard, under her lee, was a huge rock, the seas just breaking over it, and one of the ship's boats surging about at deck level, both of which made an approach there very awkward.

By this time the lifesaving team on top of the cliffs were using their searchlight and this gave Coxswain Allchorn some assistance in gauging his approach. Earlier in the evening a piece of flotsam had fouled the starboard propeller and bent the shaft so that engine was not giving full revolutions, an additional problem. The coxswain started his run in, shaving past the outer edge of the huge rock and then swinging sharply in towards the *Germania* to dodge a reef of rock closer in-shore. Twice the lifeboat bumped heavily on the bottom, she was tossing wildly but in she came, her bows up against the side of the wreck. Ropes were flung form the wreck, the lifeboatmen tried to hold her in position alongside a rope ladder, Coxswain Allchorn used the engines very skilfully, to keep her nosing up all the time and Mechanic Michael Hardy was nursing the engines to give maximum power. After about ten minutes in a most difficult situation all the 16 men on the wreck were taken off and Coxswain Allchorn was able to bring the *Beryl Tollemache* clear without further damage.

For this courageous and skilful service Coxswain Allchorn was awarded the Bronze Medal of the R.N.L.I., and the Institution's thanks on vellum was awarded to Mechanic Michael Hardy.

In spite of improved ship designs and mechanical aids to navigation, there seemed to be an astonishing increase in the number of services at Eastbourne as with so many other stations. In April 1958 it was the fishing boat *Indian Summer*, with her trawl entangled in her propeller in difficulty in Pevensey Bay. The motor yacht *Winifred* had an engine failure off Beachy Head in a south-westerly gale in April the following year and had to be towed to Newhaven.

By 1961 John Bassett took over as coxswain and in September had to feel his way in thick fog to the tanker *British Aviator* which had collided with the *Crystal Jewel*. He took the 31 strong crew of the latter vessel off the tanker which had picked them up and then had the utmost difficulty in reaching shore again having to be guided in by maroons fired off at intervals from the boat-house.

After being re-engined with twin diesels the *Beryl Tollemache* was soon out on service again in April 1963 to a ship on fire, the *Aghios Georgios II* of Beirut. The crew and captain's wife had already been taken off by other vessels so they were transferred to the lifeboat which brought them ashore. Hastings lifeboat, the *MTC*, also stood by in case of need.

Further calls from small boats suggested the need for an Inshore Lifeboat at this station, so an I.L.B. was brought into operation in 1964.

In September of that year a call came to the motor boat *Jean Luc* listing in heavy seas. She was lashed to the lifeboat to avoid her sinking and towed into Newhaven.

On the 15th July, 1965 there came yet another collision in fog when the Liberian motor vessel *Francesca* and the Greek steamer *Nymfea* collided over ten miles off Beachy Head, the latter vessel being holed and seriously damaged. Several other ships in the area went to her assistance and when the *Beryl Tollemache* arrived 27 survivors were transferred to her while the captain and three other members of her crew remained aboard waiting for a tug.

To detail the list of all the overturned dinghies, cabin cruisers and other small craft assisted would be tedious, but in nearly every instance seamanship of a high order was required. Sometimes it was the I.L.B. working close inshore and launched in a matter of a few minutes but it was the *Beryl Tollemache* that was involved in a most unusual mission which led to the Thanks of the Institution inscribed on vellum being awarded to Coxswain Michael Bassett.

At 11.46 a.m. on 11th May, 1966 a telephone message from the police to the Honorary Secretary reported that a lighthouse keeper at Beachy Head Lighthouse had injured his legs and needed treatment in hospital. At once the R.A.F. Station at Thorney was alerted and a helicopter was sent out, but in view of the weather conditions, a squally south-south-westerly force 5 to 6 wind with a fairly rough sea, it was agreed that the lifeboat should launch as well. In these gusty winds the helicopter could not take the man off, so instead one of her crewmen was lowered onto the *Beryl Tollemache* with a stretcher. Now came the really difficult part. Coxswain Bassett approached the lighthouse landing stage noticing that on the western side a heavy swell was breaking. He therefore approached the eastern side letting go his anchor and dropping astern on the cable, turning the lifeboat head to sea with a bridle from her port quarter. Ropes from the lighthouse landing stage were then made fast fore and aft to warp her in. First one parted and had to be re-secured, then the other — it was a tricky job, for the lifeboat was surging about in the heavy swell and the coxswain had to try to hold her in position by using his engines. Choosing a smoother moment he came in right alongside but despite his consummate skill several stanchions and three feet of the fender were damaged as the keepers lowered their injured colleague, who weighed 21 stone, into the boat. He was finally landed at Eastbourne at 4.07 p.m.

One final escorting service may be mentioned as it occurred again in a very rough sea and involved the difficult task of transferring men and women into the tossing and ranging lifeboat. It was a 9.45 p.m. on 7th January, 1967 that it was learned that a German motor ship, the *Saale*, was on fire and needing assistance. The *Beryl Tollemache* launched into the night in a fresh east-south-easterly wind and went alongside the vessel which was south of Beachy Head. Here it was learned that most of the crew had been taken off by the tanker *Edenfield*, so Derek Huggett, who had now taken over as coxswain, brought the lifeboat alongside the tanker, taking off 12 crew and transferring them to the *Saale* to help fight the fire. He returned to the *Edenfield*, came alongside again and took off 14 more crew and a woman. By this time tugs were on the scene so the *Beryl Tollemache* took the survivors ashore while, in turn, the Newhaven, Shoreham and Selsey boats escorted the ship till she was finally beached near Spithead. It sounds a relatively simple service but anyone who has tried to bring a boat alongside in a heavy swell will appreciate the skill required especially at night.

With a station record of one gold, one silver and three bronze gallantry medals, 370 lives saved since the R.N.L.I. took over the station and a further 50 people rescued by the Inshore Lifeboat, in its first 10 years, Eastbourne may well be proud of its lifeboats.

One final point should be made about Eastbourne. At the naming ceremony of the *Beryl Tollemache* in 1949 there was also unveiled a plaque recording that the electric clock on the lifeboat house was a memorial to two former Presidents of the Ladies' Lifeboat Guild, Mrs Astley Roberts and Mrs Muspratt Williams. The Eastbourne Branch and the Ladies' Lifeboat Guild have been tireless throughout the years in promoting the interests of the R.N.L.I. and like Margate and Walmer have covered the annual expenses of their boat with surplus going to R.N.L.I. funds.

CHAPTER EIGHT

SEAFORD BAY

Newhaven, Brighton and Shoreham

THE busy port of Newhaven, at the mouth of the River Ouse, was known as Meeching Haven in the seventeenth century, for in those days it was the village of Meeching. The steady eastward drift of shingle along the coast, which had caused the silting up of New Romney, Rye and Winchelsea and, further north, the port of Sandwich, in Tudor times blocked the mouth of the Ouse at Seaford but the river burst its banks and carved a straight route seaward forming a new haven.

Trade soon built up as this was the port for Lewes and shipbuilding and repair work were soon a feature of the place. Mr John Julius Angerstein, Chairman of Lloyds, suggested in the early 1800s that £2,000 should be set aside for the provision of lifeboats at places of particular danger, a Greathead boat being provided for Newhaven in 1803.

Even before this date, however, the local people were agitating to have a lifeboat or at least some means of saving the crews of shipwrecked vessels because of the large number of craft going ashore under the precipitous cliffs to the westward. What really brought this need to everyone's notice was the appalling disaster in 1800 when a Royal Navy ship, H.M.S. *Brazen*, piled up on the rocks in the vicinity, Captain Hanson and 104 of his crew being drowned, a sole survivor reaching shore alive. There is a memorial to these tragic sailors in St Michael's churchyard.

A local committee was promptly formed, and the 22 foot long boat built by Greathead of South Shields was stationed here, as mentioned above but there seems to be some doubt as to whether she was ever launched on service. She is, however, recorded as having been transferred to Brighton in 1809.

The local committee looked into ways and means of making better use of the lifeboat, perhaps due to her being kept too far up-river or because the design was not suited to the crew and they decided to order another lifeboat designed and built by Christopher Wilson. A Mr Langridge sponsored this boat which was named *Adeline* but it is not known for certain where she was kept or for how long she remained. At this time the harbour was still just a tidal basin with a most formidable bar choking up the mouth, and heavily laden vessels often had to off-load part of their cargo into barges before they could enter.

Adeline appears to have been here from 1802 but we know definitely that the local committee purchased an 18 foot × 6¼ foot boat from William Plenty of Newbury for the sum of £90. The R.N.L.I. had a hand in the order and probably made a contribution to the cost. She pulled four oars and was on station from 1825, but again there are no records of her services but she was laid up in 1829 and allowed to rot away.

Spanish barque *Vizcaya* towed into Newhaven by the steamer *Lyons*, lifeboat *Friend in Need* escorting, 1859.   *A. S. Payne*

One of the features of the boats built by Plenty was the arrangement of six scuppers or draining valves which assisted in clearing the boats of water. They were very broad amidships and had a thick cork lining on the bottom to give protection on stony beaches but the boats were not self-righting.

The first lifeboat to feature in the R.N.L.I.'s official records was presented to the town in 1852 and served until 1863. She was a 29 foot × 7 foot 3 inch self-righter, pulling ten oars and built by James Beeching of Yarmouth, stationed at Newhaven by the Shipwrecked Fishermen and Mariners Society. She was named *Friend in Need*, taken over by the R.N.L.I. when all the Shipwrecked Mariners were absorbed in 1854, and modified to Peake's design in 1857. During her eleven years on station she launched six times rescuing nine lives, the crew also joining in the saving of the Spanish barque *Vizcaya* in February 1859. This ship must have been in collision out in the Channel for her masts, spars and rigging were lying about her in utter confusion, her bulwarks were stove in, ship's boats smashed and absolutely no sign of the crew. Thanks to the efforts of Rottingdean Coastguards, the steamer *Lyons* and the Newhaven lifeboat she was safely brought into harbour. During these years there began one of those amazing family connections with the lifeboat, a connection which was to last for a hundred years, when the first of the Winter family joined her crew in 1854.

In 1863 she was replaced by the *Thomas Chapman*, a boat originally built by Beeching in 1852 but lengthened by Forrestt in 1862. She was a 35 foot × 8 foot self-righter, pulling twelve oars, but was only engaged in two services before her place was taken by a second *Thomas Chapman* in 1867. This boat, a 33 foot × 8 foot self-righter and built by Forrestt, was re-named *Elizabeth Boys* in 1870, the lifeboat house being re-built and other alterations made to accommodate the new boat. With her the tally of launches made and lives saved began to increase. In 1875, for example, when the barque *Margaret Evans* of Glasgow was caught in a strong south-westerly gale, she was launched and stood by the vessel for hours when it stranded on the rocks below Seaford Head. As the weather grew worse the crew of 20 were finally taken off by the lifeboat and brought safely into Newhaven.

Rescue work was not limited to the lifeboat crew for ten men put out in a small boat in 1871, to rescue the crew of two of the French lugger *Conciliator* of Nantes which stranded 100 yards eastward of the pier.

In 1877 after rescuing 26 the *Elizabeth Boys* was replaced by the first of a series of boats named *Michael Henry*, all of them the gift of the Jewish Scholars lifeboat fund. She was built by Woolfe, a 37 foot × 8½ foot self-righter pulling twelve oars and one year later, 1878, her Coxswain E. Muett was drowned but not when he was on lifeboat service. The sad accident occurred aboard his barge whilst on passage from Lewes to Newhaven. After five service launches during which seven lives were saved the *Michael Henry* was replaced by *Michael Henry*, ON 211, which was on station from 1881 to 1897. During nearly the whole of her spell of duty Richard Lower was coxswain and again this is a family with long connections with the lifeboat for Charles Lower was bowman at that time and young Dick Lower was with the crew on the famous service to the *Mogens Koch* in 1929.

Michael Henry (ON 211) was a 37 foot × 9 foot self-righter built by Woolfe and with her the number of services increased dramatically. So did her dangers for when she was launched to the brig *Harriet* of Newhaven on 26th November, 1881, she was just returning to her station when a very heavy sea struck her port side and she capsized but fortunately without loss of life.

In 1887 she was called to the Norwegian barque *New Brunswick* in trouble near Birling Gap in a furious southerly gale. She took off the crew, despite mountainous seas, and later was able to bring the ship into Newhaven. With 30 service launches and 24 lives saved she was withdrawn in favour of *Michael Henry*, ON 407, which, under Coxswain George Winter, performed many notable services.

The second *Michael Henry*, at Newhaven 1881-1897.   *A. S. Payne*

Above—Crew of the fourth *Michael Henry*. One man is still wearing corks, the remainder are in Kapok lifejackets which were introduced in 1906. Below—Crew of *Sir Fitzroy Clayton*, about 1920.

A. S. Payne

She was a heavier boat than the others, a self-righter of 37 foot × 9 foot 3 inch, built by Thames Ironworks and weighing 4 tons 12 cwt.

One of the reasons for the great increase in services was the growing importance of Newhaven. There was a flourishing shipbuilding and repair industry, the London Brighton and South Coast Railway Company had started the profitable Newhaven-Dieppe cross-channel service and there were cargo ships plying between Newhaven, Caen, St Nazaire and south to the Mediterranean ports or north to the Baltic. In fact Newhaven had become one of the most important ports in the south of England, prospering because of its shipping interests.

One of the *Michael Henry's* (ON 407) earlier services was to the barque *Peruvian* bound for Hamburg which ran aground in a whole gale on the night of 8th February, 1899. She was close in, just opposite the Esplanade Hotel, and efforts were made by the local Coastguards to put a line aboard by means of the rocket-apparatus and so save the crew by breeches-buoy. The high wind which caused the rockets to fly wide helped the *Michael Henry*, ON 407, which Coxswain Winter had launched, to cross the bay swiftly. With great skill the lifeboat was worked in between the wreck and the shore, a line was put aboard and one by one the nine men were brought to safety. After landing them at Newhaven Coxswain Winter put out again to stand by the stricken vessel, being towed part of the way by the tug *Nelson*. The lifeboatmen were utterly exhausted by their efforts although there were still two men on board. The Coastguards had now managed to put a line onto the wreck and prepared to haul these two survivors ashore through the surf. One was brought over safely, but the other had just climbed out of the breeches-buoy when he was knocked over by a huge wave, swept away and lost.

In 1904 the *J. McConnel Hussey* of Folkestone was sent, as we have seen, to Newhaven for sea trials with her new petrol engine and so successful were these that it was decided to equip the *Michael Henry*, ON 407, with a similar engine. She went back to Thames Ironworks for a long re-fit, a 4 cylinder Thorneycroft engine developing 24 b.h.p. was installed. During her absence a reserve boat, the *Quiver No 1* (formerly at Margate) was on station; and on 2nd November, 1905, at 7.15 a.m., she launched to a steamer in distress four miles to the east of the harbour. In a south-westerly gale, with a heavy sea running, she found the *Millgate* of Manchester with a severe list to port, her cargo having shifted. After standing by for half an hour it was clear that the ten people on board were in grave danger so the lifeboat worked close in and rescued them. Less than an hour later the steamer suddenly turned completely over and foundered. Special monetary rewards were made to the lifeboatmen for a smart service in heavy seas.

On 13th March, 1906 when proceeding to a French fishing smack, TR 47, stranded a quarter of a mile to the eastward, a heavy sea struck one of the oars so violently that it threw the oarsman overboard but fortunately he was picked up none the worse.

After exhaustive trials the *Michael Henry II* was returned to Newhaven and as the first motor lifeboat at this station continued her wonderful record of launches

Naming ceremony of motor lifeboat *Sir Fitzroy Clayton* on station 1912 to 1930. Note she was launched stern first.

A. S. Payne

and rescues, one of the first being to the s.s. *Trouville* of Newhaven on 6th March, 1908. In a south by west gale with a big sea running the steamer got broadside on to the bar outside the harbour. The lifeboat launched, helped to put a line aboard from a tug and then stood by while the ship was towed clear. The weather was very bad but both the boat and the engine were reported to have behaved splendidly. Another was the long and praiseworthy service to the P & O liner *Oceana* mentioned in the previous chapter. The captain of the *Oceana* wrote to the national press and the R.N.L.I. praising the wonderful work of the lifeboats in helping his ship and passengers, mentioning the Newhaven boat in particular.

In 1912 with the steadily growing importance of Newhaven it was decided that a specially built motor lifeboat should be provided, faster and more reliable than any of its fore-runners. The *Michael Henry II* was withdrawn after rescuing a total of 105 lives, first as a pulling and sailing boat and then equipped with a motor — a very splendid record. Her replacement, only two years before the First World War, was the *Sir Fitzroy Clayton*, ON 628, which was named at Newhaven by Lady Brassey. Built by Thames Ironworks she was a motor self-righter, 38 foot × 9 foot 9 inch, weighing 8 tons 15 cwt and costing £3,981. Except for a brief spell when she was sent to the Lizard between May 1918 and January 1919 and her customary absences for overhaul, she was at Newhaven until 1930 being very highly regarded by her Coxswain Dick Payne and the crew.

A contemporary picture of her shows an open lifeboat with high end-boxes, mast and tackle for sail and a small cowling or shelter just aft of amidships over the engine controls. She was steered by a wheel just forward of the rear end box. In fact, although classed as a motor self-righter, she was really a traditional pulling and sailing lifeboat with an auxiliary engine. This was not really the case in action of course. The 6 cylinder Tyler engine proved most reliable throughout the large number of launches during her 18 years, no previous lifeboat coming anywhere near her figure of 66 services. Very often it was a case of standing by some ship aground on the bar until she refloated, or of assisting in putting tow-ropes aboard to bring off a casualty. Many of the services were to fishing boats and, of course, during the First World War she was out to vessels mined or torpedoed. But a few years after the war came a service which proved to the full the unsinkable quality of the boat and the courage and seamanship of her coxswain and crew.

On 27th November, 1924 the cross-channel steamer *Dieppe* ran aground between four and five o'clock in the morning as she was entering Newhaven harbour in a strong south-westerly gale. At once two of the harbour tugs, the *Alert* and the *Richmere*, put out to her assistance, but the smaller of them, the *Richmere*, herself got into trouble and started to sink near the Promenade steps. The lifeboat had launched to stand by the *Dieppe* but, on learning of the *Richmere's* plight, Coxswain Dick Payne brought the *Sir Fitzroy Clayton* alongside the tug just as she was settling down. In the nick of time he took off Captain Weller and his three men but at that moment the *Richmere* rolled over smashing the lifeboat's gunwale and making a gaping hole in her side. True to her design, however, the lifeboat did not sink. The rescued tug men were landed and the *Sir Fitzroy Clayton* put out again into the wilderness of stormy seas to stand by the *Dieppe* until she was refloated.

The bronze medal of the R.N.L.I. was awarded to Coxswain Payne for this very skilful and gallant service in a whole gale, and the Thanks of the Institution inscribed on vellum to each member of the crew. The Southern Railway, the owners of the *Dieppe*, made a donation to the funds of the R.N.L.I. to show their appreciation.

Dick Payne who had joined the lifeboat as a boy of sixteen in the *Michael Henry*, ON 407, under George Winter had a wonderful team with him on this service. Second Coxswain Rocky Clarke was a great pal of his, Ernie Cantell, the mechanic, was a boatbuilder who tended the boat and engine with such care that she never failed them, Fred Payne was bowman and in the crew were Ben French, the Holder Brothers, the Winters and Dick Lower the youngest member. There were many others at various times, boatbuilders, coal porters working at the railway company's wharf to re-fuel the mail boats, fishermen and most of them from families that had long connection with the boat.

It was this band of men who were involved in a most gruelling service on the night of 6th/7th December, 1929. All along the south coast the gale raged with incredible ferocity throughout the hours of darkness, gusts of 110 m.p.h. being recorded, and it was not long before vessels were in difficulty in these conditions. An S.O.S. from the Hungarian steamer *Honved* sent the Selsey boat hurtling into the night to search unavailingly, but so bad were the seas on her return that she had to

Coxswain William Harvey of Newhaven.
R.N.L.I.

ride the gale out off-shore, her crew at last being able to land 12 hours after launching. Shoreham's new boat *Samuel Oakes* answered the same call battling with the same desperate conditions till 5.35 a.m. The Dutch steamer *Merwede* went aground off Newhaven and was responsible for the first service of the night for the Newhaven crew. Then, in the early hours of the morning, came the second call for her, this time from the Danish motor schooner *Mogens Koch*. She was a four-masted vessel and was reported ashore by the Birling Gap Coastguards. She had in fact brought up, with flooded engine room and a heavy list, just east of Cuckmere Haven, but her anchors dragged and she piled up on the shore, swinging round as she struck so that the breakers were making a clean breach over her deck.

As the lifeboat left the harbour and started across Seaford Bay the crew realised that conditions were far worse than they had been on their earlier service. When they neared the *Mogens Koch* they dropped anchor and veered down on the cable towards the wreck, but the breakers thundering in and recoiling caught them and swept them clear. A second time they tried but were again defeated by the swirling waves. However, at the third attempt Coxswain Payne managed with great skill to bring the lifeboat close under the bows of the wreck, every one of the ten crew members leaping down to safety.

It was as they were punching into the seas on the return journey that disaster almost overtook the lifeboat. An enormous wave suddenly overwhelmed her, smashing the engine shelter, flinging everyone violently off their feet and filling the boat with foaming water. The second mechanic Fred Holder was washed right out of her but by the greatest luck, his foot caught in a snarled up tangle of rope and he was pulled back on board. One man had a broken hip, another a fractured jaw, and gallant Dick Payne who had been dashed against the stern had the worst injury of all, a broken pelvis. In spite of this he refused to hand over the helm until he had brought the *Sir Fitzroy Clayton* back into harbour, and had landed the rescued.

For his skill, judgement and high courage the R.N.L.I. awarded Coxswain Payne the silver medal for gallantry, and all members of the crew were awarded the Thanks of the Institution inscribed on vellum. The King of Denmark also awarded an inscribed gold watch to the coxswain and silver goblets to each member of the crew in recognition of their heroism.

Unhappily, the injuries he received forced Dick Payne to retire in 1930 and caused his death in June, 1931 deeply mourned by the people of Newhaven and all his lifeboat comrades.

This same year, 1930, saw *Sir Fitzroy Clayton* withdrawn after rescuing 108 lives, a new Watson cabin motor lifeboat, the *Cecil & Lilian Philpott*, ON 730, taking her place. This new lifeboat, 45 foot 6 inch × 12 foot 6 inch, was built by J. Samuel White of Cowes, and weighed 19 tons 12 cwt. She was in every way a vast improvement on the old boat, with twin 40 h.p. engines, a radius of action of 120 miles and capable of taking aboard 100 persons, and was christened by His Royal Highness Prince George. With her advent the number of services increased still further and in her 19 years she not only went across to Dunkirk but also launched 154 times saving a total of 99 lives.

One of her finest services was to assist H.M. trawler *Avanturine* in 1943 when Coxswain Len Peddlesden was awarded the silver medal for gallantry and bronze medals were awarded to the other seven members of the crew. The full story of this war-time service is told in Chapter Ten.

Bill Harvey took over as coxswain in 1948 and was involved in a number of meritorious services, one of which resulted in another award for gallantry. Once again a Danish auxiliary schooner, the *Vega*, was involved. It was on 27th November,

Brighton lifeboat *William Wallis* being launched early in the 1900s.

From an old postcard. R.N.L.I.

Shoreham lifeboat *William Restell* (ON 276) returning from a service. *C. M. Ayling*

1950 and a whole gale was blowing from the south-south-west, the seas being so tremendous that to bring the lifeboat safely out of harbour was, in itself, a fine feat of seamanship. The schooner was listing so heavily that it was impossible for the *Cecil & Lilian Philpott* to go alongside but working in close the coxswain and his men were able to get a line aboard her with the line-throwing gun. Then rigging the breeches-buoy they were able to take off all the crew. Almost the worst part of the service was in battling back against the gale to Newhaven, and it was three hours before the lifeboat was back at her station and the rescued men safely ashore.

For his skill and courage the silver medal for gallantry was awarded to Coxswain Bill Harvey, and he also received the Maud Smith award for the bravest act of life-saving during the year.

With the retirement in 1954 of the second coxswain, S. Winter, the one hundred year old family record was broken, for ever since 1854 there had always been a Winter in the boat.

Among the *Cecil & Lilian Philpott's* many other services were the Belgian trawler *Celtic* which sank two miles off Newhaven on 9th April, 1958, to tow in the yacht *Topaz* which had a broken rudder, and to escort the motor yacht *Santa Maria* in difficulties off Rottingdean in 1959. Finally in 1959 she was replaced by the present lifeboat *Kathleen Mary*, ON 950, a 47 foot × 13 foot Watson cabin type, weighing 22 tons 11 cwt, built by Osborne's of Littlehampton and costing the large sum of £34,500, a matter of £27,000 more than the previous boat. This splendidly equipped boat has already made over 300 services launches, saving more lives than any of her predecessors, many of her missions being to yachts in difficulties or fishing boats with engine failure as on 23rd June, 1963 when she towed in the *Silver Wings*, and 4th August, 1966 when she guided the Dutch fishing vessel *Guus* into harbour.

None of these launches presented any great hazard, yet in nearly every case a vessel and the people on board might have been in grave danger had the lifeboat not been at hand; and all required the experienced seamanship which the crews at Newhaven have shown so splendidly over more than 150 years, winning ten silver and nine bronze medals for gallantry during this time. It is appropriate, too, to mention the M.B.E. conferred upon the Station's Honorary Secretary, Mr R. K. Sayer, for his long and conspicuous service to Newhaven. In 1977 the Round Table celebrated their fiftieth anniversary by presenting a new Waveney type boat for Newhaven to be named *Louis Marchesi of Round Table* in memory of the founder of the movement.

Some ten miles westward is the wide-spreading tourist centre of Brighton which was once the little fishing village of Brighthelmston. Like so many other seaside towns it began to prosper with the vogue for sea-bathing in the middle eighteenth century; Dr Russell of Lewes began the sea-bathing and medical spring cures that aided the development of the modern health report. With the patronage of the Prince Regent and the building of the famous, if bizarre, Royal Pavilion, the fashionable quality of the place was confirmed and the seal was set to its prosperity by the opening of the London to Brighton railway in 1841.

The local townsfolk seem to have been aware of the need for a lifeboat early in the nineteenth century for in 1809 the Greathead boat which had been at Newhaven was transferred here. However she was reported to be unsuitable and was probably not used. Nevertheless in the first Annual Report of the R.N.L.I.,* 1825 it was noted that "local associations which have affiliated themselves with this Institution, have been formed at the following places: — Dover, Brighton, Penzance, Newcastle on Tyne, and Bridlington".

The next local affiliated boat of which we have a record is one that was at Brighton from 1825 to 1837. However, it is known that Captain Saumarez R.N., one of the Committee of the Institution, came down to Brighton specifically to take this boat out in a heavy sea to find out just how she would behave. She was 20 foot × 6 foot 9 inch built by William Plenty, pulling six oars, but there do not seem to be any records in existence of her services. She was removed to Scilly in 1837. Then followed a 28 foot 3 inch × 6 foot 9 inch boat by Tayler to Palmer's design which was on station until 1854, then being sold to a Mr John Wright who owned pleasure boats and bathing machines and who made use of her as a private lifeboat until 1858. The Peake adaptation of Beeching's prize winning boat was towed down to Brighton by an Admiralty tug in February, 1852. She was under the command of Captain Ross Ward and had a crew of coastguards. Among those watching her performance on trial was James Beeching and the Duke of Northumberland, President of the R.N.L.I. from 1851-65, who was determined to cover the complete

*Then the National Institution for the Preservation of Life from Shipwreck.

Shoreham lifeboat *William Restell* (the second) on her launching trolley, drawn by horses.

C. M. Ayling

Northumbrian coast with suitable boats at his own cost. The trials turned out to be very successful as she behaved well off-shore and brought the crew to the beach through heavy rollers without shipping any water. In 1840 the Town Authorities had a further boat built by Johnston of Hove at a cost of £60. She was a 22½ foot × 6½ foot, pulling four or six oars and it was these two boats that went out to the assistance of the brig *Pilgrim* which was laden with a cargo of coal for Portsmouth and was in difficulties in October, 1857. John Wright's boat was manned by his own four men plus four coastguards, but the town authority seems to have made no special provision for a crew. Their boat would be handled by such fishermen as were near at hand when the alarm was given.

From 1858 to 1867 the first R.N.L.I. boat was stationed here, a 30 foot × 7½ foot self-righter built by Forrestt. During this time she was launched from the beach on three occasions but was not responsible for saving any lives.

In 1867 a 33 foot × 8 foot 10 inch built by Forrestt came on duty here. She was particularly interesting as the money for her building was collected by the children of the Sunday Schools of London who raised altogether the splendid sum of £580, £280 of which went to the cost of this boat, the balance being reserved for a second one. The boat was duly named *Robert Raikes* after the founder of the Sunday School movement but she only had one recorded service launch, probably because, according to the Board of Trade's Wreck Register, most of the casualties in this area were well out at sea and more easily reached by the lifeboats from Newhaven or from further westward along the coast, Selsey for example.

The second *Robert Raikes* 32 foot × 7 foot 8 inch was built by Woolfe from the balance of the Sunday School fund and came on station in 1874. Again her number of service launches was small, but the sight of the lifeboat must have been a reassurance and a great interest to the crowds of holiday-makers for it is interesting to note that the old-style collecting boxes on the piers brought in an annual sum of £20.

It was during this spell of service of the second *Robert Raikes* that a great deal of beach work was undertaken by Brighton Corporation with the construction of new groynes and the R.N.L.I. agreed to take over two arches under the Western Esplanade for use as their lifeboat house and store.

In 1888 *Sunlight No 2*, ON 145, presented by Lever Brothers, took over duty and she was a self-righter, 34 foot × 7½ foot, built by Hansen of Cowes but at the same time the Brighton Corporation also had an eight oared Whale boat on the beach. This boat, the *Jane Whittingham*, provided additional safeguard for anglers and holiday makers right up to 1932. When the ketch *Antelope* was stranded off Brighton in 1904, the coxswain took out the *Jane Whittingham* with six of the lifeboat crew and five other volunteers to rescue the three men on board.

After only three service launches, although many practice displays and launches were made to interest the public, *Sunlight No 2* was withdrawn in 1904 and the last Brighton lifeboat came on the scene. Thames Ironworks built the *William Wallis*, ON 539, the gift of Mr Wallis of Brighton who left in his will £1,000 expressly for the purpose of providing a lifeboat for his home town, and she was here until the station closed in 1931. A self-righter of 35 foot × 8½ foot, she was another pulling and sailing lifeboat, with ten oars and by far the most active of the boats, being launched 23 times and saving 16 lives. There is an interesting account* of her naming ceremony when "the Lifeboat and carriage were then wheeled to the water's edge, the members of the guard of honour manned the ropes and with 'a long pull and a strong pull' hauled her off the carriage, and she slid gracefully out upon the waters amid a round of cheering from the assembled multitude".

In 1931 the station was closed with a record of 34 launches and 22 lives saved, one gold and six silver medals having been awarded to Brighton men and the motor lifeboat from Shoreham then provided adequate cover for the area. But in 1965, with the great increase in incidents concerned with bathers and small pleasure-boats an Inshore Lifeboat was stationed here. Within two years Letters of Thanks were awarded to the Crewmen G. Wheeler and E. C. Newman for their service on 15th June, 1967 when they saved a rubber dinghy and the five occupants. In its first nine years the Inshore Lifeboat rescued 42 lives in 100 launches.

Before leaving Brighton and Hove mention must be made of the R.N.L.I.'s greatest benefactor, Major Osman Gabriel of Hove, whose gift to the Institution amounted to some £200,000, thus providing both the *Osman Gabriel* and the *Mary Gabriel* lifeboats. With his great interest in the sea and the work of the R.N.L.I. it was appropriate that his death in 1974 should occur at sea, on a voyage to South Africa.

The Shoreham station which now covers the area of Brighton and Hove was inaugurated by the Shoreham Harbour Commissioners in 1845 with a 30 foot × 8

*Lifeboat Journal of 1905.

foot 9 inch boat pulling twelve oars. This was very probably one of the Liverpool type boats so much favoured by the port authorities there, carrying two spritsails and a jib and given additional buoyancy by means of airtight cases secured along the sides of the boat.

Shoreham itself at the mouth of the Adur is a place of considerable antiquity, with a long seafaring tradition going back to Norman times. At the time of the Hundred Years' War it assisted King Edward with 26 ships, it was from this place that Charles II made his famous escape after the battle of Worcester in Captain Tattersell's collier brig, and warships were built here as late as the beginning of the eighteenth century. A considerable amount of yacht and boat building has continued, with coal and timber trade as well, but the harbour has always been plagued by the eastward drift of shingle which played such havoc with so many of our south coast ports. It is for this reason that the lifeboat station has been shifted from time to time, to make it easier for the boat to clear the somewhat difficult entrance in high seas.

The Harbour Commissioner's lifeboat served here for twenty years until 1865 during which time she appears to have saved two lives although details are lacking. She was then replaced by the *Ramonet*, ON 212, the first of the R.N.L.I. boats which was a 33 foot × 8 foot self-righter built by Forrestt, and costing £286. In order to accommodate her a new lifeboat house was specially constructed at Kingston, near the present one, and in 1870 the Harbour Commissioners added a slip from the boathouse to the water's edge to facilitate the launching. It is sad to reflect that the only lifeboatman lost at Shoreham was drowned on an exercise launch in December, 1874 when an enormous sea struck her just as she was turning in broken waters on the harbour bar. The boat capsized before driving onto the beach and Robert Brazier, a member of the crew, was drowned in spite of the gallant efforts of Mr W. T. G. Sheader, a Customs Officer, who swam out through the surf at great risk to try to rescue him. The silver medal for gallantry was awarded to Mr Sheader for his brave endeavours.

During her twenty-five years on station the *Ramonet* was only launched three times on service, rescuing 12 lives, 6 from a cutter, the *Wisdom* and six from the schooner *Charles Elisa* which was driving into the bay in a south-south-westerly gale. The lifeboatmen managed to put a line aboard this vessel which was then bent to the hawser of the tug *Stella* which was thus enabled to bring the schooner safely into harbour. During these years the station was shifted to the west side of the harbour near the Coastguard Station and a little later in 1903 had to be shifted further back to a safe distance from the sea, the launching then being by a carriage drawn by horses.

This was the situation when the *William Restell*, ON 276, a 34 foot × 7½ foot self-righter built by Woolfe, came to Shoreham. Between 1890 and 1903 she launched twelve times rescuing nine lives. One of these services, in a southerly gale and rough sea, was to the barquentine *Atlantic* of Arendal which was at anchor off the harbour when she started to drag. The lifeboat was launched and, coming alongside as she struck, rescued the crew of nine who were later landed at Brighton as a shift of the wind made it difficult to return to Shoreham.

Her successor *William Restell II*, ON 532, built by Thames Ironworks was again a self-righter, 35 foot × 8 foot 8 inch and was on station from 1904 to 1924. She made 12 service launches like her namesake, several of which involved fine seamanship in very heavy weather. On 15th March, 1905 there was a blustering south-wester in the midst of which the barque *Liburna* of Arendal stranded at about 5 p.m. The *William Restell II* was launched in a hailstorm and taken in tow by the harbour tug which brought her to windward of the wreck. She then veered down but despite the greatest care was seriously damaged as she drew alongside. All the ten men of the crew were safely taken off, after which the harbour tug took the lifeboat in tow again and brought her back into harbour.

In 1910, with the expiry of the lease of the lifeboat house on the west side, the station was moved back to the old site at Kingston and it was from here that the *William Restell II* put to sea, again in tow of the tug, on 6th August. An Italian barque, the *Amirac*, had stranded off Littlehampton in colossal seas whipped up by a south-westerly gale and started to drive up-channel quite out of control. The Littlehampton boat ranged alongside, taking off nine of the crew, but the rest refused to leave. By this time the Worthing lifeboat had arrived and stood by, presently taking off a further two men. When the *William Restell* came on the scene under tow of the tug, the captain realised that his ship might be saved. Four of the lifeboatmen went aboard the barque to assist with the tow-rope, the *William Restell* helped to connect the tow and the tug brought the ship safely into Shoreham escorted by the lifeboat.

By October, 1924 there was such serious silting in the harbour that the station had to be closed but in 1929 the bar that had blocked the entrance had been cleared so another boat, this time a motor lifeboat, was sent to reopen the station. She was the *Samuel Oakes*, ON 651, built in 1918 by Summers and Payne, a 40 foot × 11 foot Watson, weighing 10 tons. Previously she had been on station at the Humber from 1919 to 1923 and and at Weymouth until 1929 so she had already seen much service. She had a petrol engine giving her a speed of just over seven knots and her first call at Shoreham was in hurricane conditions. The Hungarian steamer *Honved* sent out an S.O.S. from the neighbourhood of the Owers Lightvessel on 6th December, 1929. Several of the lifeboatmen were at a concert that evening but they left hurriedly when the announcement was made from the stage. Launching into the howling gale the lifeboat searched unavailingly for some hours finally learning that the ship in distress was under way to the weary lifeboatmen headed for Shoreham again reaching harbour at 5.30 a.m. Coxswain Laker said of that night, "We received a terrible battering and were running under the water. We have been out in heavy weather but not one of us remembers such a wild night."

After being out on eleven services and saving seven lives the *Samuel Oakes* was replaced for a short spell by the *Maria*, ON 560, an earlier 40 foot Watson built by Thames Ironworks and previously at Broughty Ferry, Portpatrick and Pwllheli.

Left: Ned Laker, coxswain of the first motor lifeboat at Shoreham. As coxswain, from 1924-1940, he was considered to be outstanding in his knowledge of local waters, able to bring the boat in safely even in the pitch darkness of war-time black-out. *Right:* Coxswain Upperton of Shoreham, 1947-1957. As second coxswain he won the silver medal for gallantry for rescuing 21 crew plus the coxswain from the minesweeper *President Briand* on 16th November, 1941.
Left: C. M. Ayling. Right: Photograph by Hamlin, Brighton. R.N.L.I.

Then a new Watson, built by Groves and Guttridge, came to Shoreham and there began a tremendous series of rescues.

She was the *Rosa Woodd & Phyllis Lunn* a twin-screw motor lifeboat, 41 foot × 11 foot 8 inch, weighing 14 tons 10 cwt. To house her a new boathouse and slipway was built so that she could be launched at any state of the tide and a Royal naming ceremony was arranged for her, H.R.H. Prince George coming to Shoreham for the great occasion. In his speech he referred to the noble work of Sussex lifeboatmen recalling that since 1850 they had saved no fewer than 875 lives and had won 32 medals for gallantry. "The honour of that record," he said, "the whole country shares."

The *Rosa Woodd & Phyllis Lunn* was on station for thirty years, making 244 service launches in that time and saving altogether 143 lives including the late Right Honourable "Jimmy" Thomas, at that time Secretary of State for the Dominions who had been angling with some friends.

As well as being one of the lifeboats at the Dunkirk evacuation, she saw notable service during the war particularly when she was out for 11 hours to rescue the 21 men on board the minesweeper *President Briand*. For this service Acting Coxswain James Upperton was awarded the silver medal for gallantry, Henry Philcox the mechanic the bronze medal, and the Thanks of the Institution on vellum to the Bowman John E. Laker, Assistant-mechanic Cecil M. Ayling and Victor H. Page, Charles E. Laker and Albert E. Upperton.

On Sunday, 8th August, 1948 there was a strong south-westerly gale, the sea was very rough and there was a heavy swell. Shortly after 8.30 a.m. a yacht was sighted, her sails torn and driving up the coast out of control. The *Rosa Woodd & Phyllis Lunn* launched, crossed the bar in heavy breaking seas and set off in pursuit of the vessel, keeping up the chase for 14 miles until they were off Newhaven. The yacht *Gull* which had three men, two women and a boy on board made a desperate effort to run into harbour but gybed and the waves washed right over her sending her slewing away to leeward into the breakers. She tried to drop anchor but the cable parted and in a very few moments she would be ashore. Coxswain Upperton did not hesitate but took the lifeboat straight in despite the tremendous seas. As he did so a breaker smothered the boat and he thought he must have lost some of his men but all was well and he was able to lay the lifeboat along the weather side of the yacht in the shallows. The lifeboatmen grabbed and hauled aboard five of the six people but the coxswain had to back away and come in a second time before they could seize the last man. It was a wonderfully skilful rescue carried out in the nick of time and on a dead lee shore and the R.N.L.I. awarded the coxswain a bar to his silver medal and its Thanks on Vellum to all seven members of the crew.

During the 1950s and 1960s the types of service were changing here as elsewhere, with the vast increase in the number of launches to yachts, fishing parties, skin divers and bathers. In April 1961 for example it was the yacht *Aquilla* which had been taken in tow in a disabled condition by the Dutch steamer *Deo Gloria*. The *Rosa Woodd & Phyllis Lunn* met the steamer, took over the tow and brought the yacht and its occupants into Shoreham. In June it was a capsized sailing boat off Lancing. An Inshore Lifeboat was therefore brought on station in 1967 and in the first eight years of operation it has rescued 234 lives.

Shoreham harbour tug *Stella* which assisted in this rescue of the Italian barque *Amirac*.

C. M. Ayling

Six brothers of the Upton family, all members of the lifeboat crew at the service to the *Liburna*.

C. M. Ayling

Another Watson cabin lifeboat built by Groves and Guttridge took over the duties here, the 42 foot × 12 foot *Dorothy and Philip Constant*, ON967, which had the distinction of being shown at the 1963 Boat Show. Twin 55 h.p. Gardner diesels give her a speed of just over 8½ knots, she can travel 200 miles without refuelling and is equipped with the latest equipment for radio-telephone communication with shore and helicopter. Divided into ten watertight compartments and with a watertight engine room and further protected by a double bottom below the engines, she is wonderfully buoyant and weatherly. H.R.H. Princess Marina, the President of the R.N.L.I., came down to name her on 18th July, 1963 and before the end of the year she had been on call many times, among others to escort the coaster *Sandrunner* of Goole, which had developed a twenty degree list, into harbour.

With the Inshore Lifeboat to deal with the services to bathers and smaller boats, the *Dorothy and Philip Constant* has been used chiefly in bad weather and for night operations. But even so the average number of calls has been eleven each year. There have also been changes in the crew for with the I.L.B. as a training ground most of the volunteers are now younger men. After the retirement of Coxswain Upperton who had first joined the crew in 1910, Victor Page took over until an accident at work in the harbour forced him to give up. His brother Eric then became coxswain in 1963, with John Fox as second coxswain, Harry Philcox motor mechanic, Sid Page bowman, Cecil Ayling second mechanic, and Alf Page and Ray Pellant as crew. Then with the sad death of Coxswain E. Page in 1968, the retirement of Alf and Sid Page and also the retirement of Cecil Ayling after thirty-seven years in the boat, John Fox became coxswain with Harry Philcox second coxswain/mechanic. He is the last of the pre-war crew of the thirties and has served under six coxswains. In 1971 the B.E.M. was conferred upon him in recognition of his services to the R.N.L.I.

John Fox and his new crew carried out a splendid service on 22nd September, 1968 to the yacht *Jean Ann*, which had anchored off Littlehampton with the intention of entering the harbour on the midnight tide. The engine was out of order, she was becoming waterlogged and as the wind increased her crew could not release the anchor chain. In this distress they fired off their one and only flare at about 8 p.m. which was fortunately seen by the Coastguards at Littlehampton. The *Dorothy and Philip Constant* launched, searched the area and, locating the yacht, brought her safely to Shoreham through a heavy sea where the rescued were refreshed with rum and hot soup and put up for the night by members of the lifeboat crew. For this service the coxswain and crew were awarded a formal letter of thanks signed by the Chairman of the Institution.

Three years later, on 19th August, 1971, a far more hazardous service faced the lifeboatmen. Reports reached Shoreham that the crew of the drilling rig *William Allpress*, anchored one mile off Rustington, needed assistance. The lifeboat launched at 2.10 p.m. in very bad conditions, with a gale from the south-west, force 9 gusting up to storm force, and a heavy sea and swell. Heavy rain and mist patches made visibility poor but by 3.35 p.m. they had reached the rig which proved very difficult to approach because of its shape and the tremendous seas breaking over it. However there was a slight lee on one side so Coxswain Fox used all his fenders up at the bows and kept the lifeboat pushed up against the rig long enough for four of the five men to be hauled on board. The lifeboat was forced away before the last man could be rescued, so she had to come in a second time. Just as he was snatched to safety a huge sea lifted the bow of the lifeboat above but clear of the deck of the rig. The return to Shoreham was in torrential rain and by dead reckoning and soundings as visibility was nil. For his excellent seamanship, courage and good judgement the bronze medal for gallantry was awarded to Coxswain John Fox and the Thanks of the Institution inscribed on vellum to assistant mechanic Kenneth Everard.

On 5th August, 1973 the Bronze Second Service clasp was awarded to Coxswain Fox for a splendid rescue in a formidable north-westerly gale. The lifeboat launched at 3.15 a.m. after the Coastguard had reported a red rocket three miles south of Littlehampton. With the aid of parachute flares and answering signals the lifeboat found the 30 foot yacht *Albin Ballad* broached to, her sails flapping in the water, the three men aboard seasick and exhausted, and waves were breaking over her. As the men seemed unable to help, Ken Everard and G. Tugwell volunteered to board her. Coxswain Fox brought the lifeboat in close, her starboard bow up against the port side of the casualty and the lifeboatmen scrambled aboard as the boats rolled together. A rope was passed and *Dorothy and Philip Constant* began to tow, but ten minutes later in a severe squall the rope parted. After some manoeuvring a second rope was passed across and they headed for the harbour. There were some awkward moments when the yacht over-ran the tow but a drogue streamed out behind steadied her. The seas on the bar were very confused with breakers creaming in from all directions and the coxswain had to use great judgement and skill in his approach, but at 7.25 a.m. the lifeboat and the yacht entered harbour safely.

In addition to the award to the coxswain the Thanks of the Institution inscribed on vellum were awarded to Ken Everard and Geoff Tugwell for their gallant service.

Unhappily only two years later John Fox died at the early age of fifty, the last surviving member of the Page family who had helped to man the Shoreham lifeboat for three generations. He had been a crew member for thirty years, of which he was second coxswain for five years and coxswain for seven.

Up to 1975 the station records show the number of launches as 479 and the lives saved 274 with Shoreham lifeboatmen having won two silver and three bronze medals for gallantry.

The Shoreham lifeboat *Samuel Oakes*, 1929.   *R.N.L.I.*

CHAPTER NINE

ENGLISH CHANNEL

Worthing, Littlehampton and Selsey

"WE'VE all done our best and if another boat comes along I think we can find another crew." So said Coxswain W. Blann at the complimentary dinner given to the lifeboat crews by the Worthing Branch of the R.N.L.I. to mark the closure of the station in 1930. The Chairman, Lieutenant Colonel A. F. Randolph, C.M.G., D.S.O., in welcoming the crews said that although Worthing was no longer an active station, their interest remained, and he was sure that their subscribers would rally round and that, from a financial point of view, things would be the same as they had been.

How right he was may be seen in the huge sums raised by the Worthing Branch and the Ladies' Lifeboat Guild, and their tireless endeavours to promote the interests of the R.N.L.I. in every way.

The station's history started when, in the great gale of 1850, the East Indiaman *Lalla Rookh* was seen lying disabled off Worthing so eleven fishermen at once put out in a boat but she capsized within sight of the shore and all the men were lost. In spite of this a second boat was launched which succeeded in reaching the *Lalla Rookh* and the fishermen helped to bring the ship safely into port. Among the crew n who became second coxswain of the lifeboat vith the idea of establishing their own lifeboat from Harvey of Littlehampton, a self-righter, for a cost of £120. This boat remained at n the R.N.L.I. took over the station in 1865. ommittee was held in the house of Admiral who was later known as Worthing's "Grand p of the local branch from 1866 until

ne, was a 32 foot × 7½ foot self-righter 880 when she was re-named *Henry Harris* n all she was launched on service eleven es was on 19th September, 1869 when a ane launched away from the shore in a rs, presently coming up with the smack re was no one on board, so some of the ught her into Worthing. It was later her moorings in the storm.

was built facing the sea and adjoining had been awkwardly placed up a

William Blann, fifty years in the Worthing lifeboat and coxswain when the station closed in 1930.   *R.N.L.I.*

side-street some distance from the shore, which made the launching of the boat a rather lengthy proceeding.

This first lifeboat was followed by the *Henry Harris II*, ON 109, which was a 34 foot × 7½ foot self-righter, built by Woolfe at a cost of £371, and which rescued 37 lives in the course of 10 services between 1887 and 1901.

Very strong family links existed with these Worthing lifeboats, as with all our south coast stations. The Bashford family had six representatives with the crews, Coxswain Dean was coxswain of the *Jane*, his son then joining the crew of the *Henry Harris* in 1884 and continuing to serve in the boat till the station closed. The second coxswain of the *Jane* was Thomas Blann whose son, Coxswain William Blann, was in the service for fifty years and coxswain when the station closed. In 1892 during an exercise launch, a member of the crew named Riddles fell down and died. He was one of only two casualties among the Worthing crews.

One of the great features of any Flag Day, or of an exercise launch, in the days before the turn of the century long before the esplanade and side-streets were thronged with cars and buses, was the spectacle of the lifeboat, mounted on its carriage, proceeding slowly down the middle of the road. The proud team of horses, the men in their long oilskins, sou'-westers and cork life-jackets, all these provided a stirring spectacle which roused great enthusiasm among holiday-makers and townsfolk alike. But the problems of launching were considerable on this gently shelving beach and though the next boat, the *Richard Coleman*, was on station from 1901 to 1930 she only launched 15 times and rescued eleven lives, seven of these being from three small motor-boats between 1920 and 1930. As recounted in the previous chapter she was out to the Italian barque *Amirac* which was driving up-Channel after the Littlehampton boat had taken off nine of her crew. The *Richard Coleman* closed with her and escorted her for some time, presently taking off a further two men by which time the Shoreham lifeboat and tug had arrived to take the vessel to safety. The *Richard Coleman*, ON 466, was 35 foot × 8½ foot, built by Thames Ironworks and weighing 3 tons 15 cwt. It was in this boat that the other fatal accident occurred on 17th February, 1915 when the lifeboat launched to the salmoner *Kingshill*. There was a strong south-westerly gale at the time and an exceptional wave flung the lifeboat onto her beam ends, the crew being thrown into the sea. They all managed to regain the boat but shortly afterwards a second wave, a monster, capsized her. When once again the exhausted and dripping men had clambered back on board it was found that crew-man E. J. Burgess was missing. He drifted ashore some little time later but all efforts to resuscitate him were in vain.

With so few calls on the lifeboat in her final ten years it was decided to close the station, but the *Richard Coleman* was kept for some time in the old boat-house as an exhibition boat of the pulling-and-sailing era.

During the 1960s the great upsurge of interest in boating led to innumerable incidents connected with air-beds floating out to sea, dinghies overturning, and inexperienced sailors bringing their boats to the coast on trailers, launching off into the deep quite regardless of the advice of local boatmen as to tidal streams and weather prospects. So, in common with Brighton, Shoreham and other seaside places an Inshore Lifeboat was stationed here in 1964. However, although there were 32 calls over the three year period, the number of lives saved, seven, did not warrant the expense of the station especially as the *Blue Peter* at nearby Littlehampton was so active.

The Littlehampton station of the R.N.L.I. was established somewhat later than those at the other Sussex ports and towns, and was prompted not so much by the activities of the local authorities or by the enthusiasm of a local committee as by the need to provide some additional protection for the various sailing vessels trading in and out of the port. So, in 1884 a boat-house was built and the *Undaunted*, which had been at Chichester Harbour (West Wittering), was moved here, complete with her launching carriage. She was a 32 foot × 7 foot 5 inch self-righting lifeboat, pulling ten oars, built by Forrestt in 1864 and over the next four years she was taken out by a crew consisting of Coastguards and fishermen but only had two service launches all told.

Worthing lifeboat *Richard Coleman* being drawn through the streets on Lifeboat Day, 2nd August, 1919.   *R.N.L.I.*

In spite of this lack of calls it was decided to replace her with a new boat the *James, Mercer and Elizabeth*, ON 172, a 34 foot × 7½ foot self-righter by Woolfe which weighed 3 tons 6 cwt. She served until 1904 being launched on ten occasions during this spell rescuing altogether twelve lives. One of these services was to a local vessel, a yawl named the *Surf*, which was caught out in a southerly gale and with the aid of the lifeboat she was brought safely into harbour.

A rather unusual and difficult rescue faced the lifeboat crew early in the morning of 11th January, 1894 when distress flares were seen close to the West Pier. There was a keen wind blowing in from the south-west at the time and they found that a brigantine from Llanelli, the *CHS* had crashed into the pier causing a great deal of damage both to herself and to the piles. One of her crew had leapt on to the pier as she struck but the remainder were still aboard the vessel which had by that time stranded in the surf. It was no easy task for the lifeboatmen to work in alongside but they succeeded, rescuing the four men.

In 1901 they had a somewhat similar problem, also in a south-westerly gale when, on the 12th November, a collier brig the *Amy* stranded to the east of the harbour. Again they had to exercise all their skill and pluck in veering in alongside her in the shallow breaking seas. They rescued the crew of six but with the wind and tide against them it was hopeless to try to beat back to the harbour. Instead they ran the *James, Mercer and Elizabeth* on to the beach some two miles from the town, landed the rescued men and later took the lifeboat back to the boathouse on her carriage.

The steamships around the turn of the century were usually single-screw vessels with reciprocating engines and sometimes they had curious and dangerous mishaps, particularly when plunging into heavy head seas. One such incident occurred on 26th February, 1903 when the steamship *Brattingsborg* of Copenhagen was seen to be flying distress signals. There was a full gale blowing at the time and the *James, Mercer and Elizabeth* tossed about wildly as she made for the casualty. Finding that the ship had lost her propeller, the lifeboat stood by for hours until a tug arrived, the unfortunate vessel was taken in tow and the lifeboatmen were able to return to harbour at 7 p.m.

The next lifeboat to be stationed here was the *Brothers Freeman*, ON 531, a 35 foot × 8½ foot self-righter built by Thames Ironworks and she was on duty from 1904 to 1921. A new lifeboat-house had been built the previous year on a different site as the Admiralty required the old one for a Coastguard station, so here the *Brothers Freeman* was duly housed. In the course of her seventeen years she launched 14 times rescuing ten people of which nine were from the drifting *Amirac* in 1912: these adventures have already been referred to under Shoreham and Worthing. It must have required very great skill to draw alongside her in such atrocious weather, especially as the ship was completely unmanageable, yawing wildly about as she drove with the giant rollers lifting her stern. Finally, in 1921, the *Brothers Freeman* was withdrawn and the station closed, having rescued a total of 22 lives in all, the area being effectively covered by the motor lifeboat at Selsey.

This was by no means the end of the story for the Littlehampton station, for in 1967 it was decided to place an Inshore Lifeboat here. As a result of the B.B.C.'s "Blue Peter" programme's appeal an I.L.B. was purchased for Littlehampton, so *Blue Peter I* re-opened the station after being on view first at the *Daily Express* Boat Show at Earl's Court.

Her first year was relatively quiet though it soon became apparent that the rapidity of launching and the speed of these Inshore Lifeboats with their powerful outboards would prove of very great value in coping with the ever-increasing number of minor casualties involving bathers, sailing-dinghies and the like. In this first year *Blue Peter I* was called out nine times rescuing two but in 1968 there were 23 calls.

On 30th May 1970 *Blue Peter I* was out in a rough sea to help the occupants of a sailing-dinghy which had capsized. She made for the scene at full speed, bounding and leaping in the swell. When the I.L.B. crew reached the up-turned boat they found a girl, cold and exhausted, clinging to it. Making a hurried search they found her companion 200 yards away so, after righting and towing the boat ashore, the two rescued were safely landed. Seventeen people were saved in 1970 and in the following year it was decided to keep the station operational all the year round.

The next stage was to bring into action a larger, more powerful boat of a design which had been developed for the R.N.L.I. at Atlantic College, St Donat's Castle in South Wales. These boats are semi-inflatables having a rigid hull below and inflatable portion above and are thus more suitable for summer and winter conditions. They also have twin outboards giving them more speed and a considerable reserve of power. How valuable this can be was seen on a service in the evening of 29th May, 1973. The Honorary Secretary was informed by the Coastguard that red flares had been sighted six miles west-south-west of the

Blue Peter Inshore Lifeboat, Atlantic 21 type, at sea off Littlehampton.   *R.N.L.I.*

harbour, whereupon the I.L.B. was launched four minutes later. The sea was only moderate but the I.L.B. crew had some difficulty in locating the casualty owing to several other craft in the area. However with further information from the shore she came up with the boat in trouble which proved to be a 30 foot fishing boat, the *Rock-'n-Roll*. A tow-line was passed but at first progress was slow due to a heavy swell. As they drew closer in-shore they made better headway and the I.L.B. completed the service, successfully bringing the fishing vessel and her crew of six to safety.

In the first eight years of operations the Littlehampton I.L.B.s have launched on service no less than 244 times rescuing 90 lives, to say nothing of the many boats towed or assisted, a startling comparison with the 26 services and 22 lives saved by the conventional lifeboats and a great credit to their keen Honorary Secretary, Mr Peter Cheney, and the skilful handling of the boat by Coxswain George Moore. Another unusual fact will be of interest. During the flood disasters of 1970 in East Pakistan two members of the lifeboat crew, C. R. Cole and C. J. Pelham, flew out there to help in training some of the local people in the use of the 20 I.R.B.s sold to the Red Cross for use in the disaster area. They were the first team of relief workers to be sent out from Britain, and were accorded the Thanks of the Institution on vellum and Certificates from the Red Cross for their efforts.

Before concluding Littlehampton it is of particular interest and pride that so many of our Kent and Sussex lifeboats have come from the Arun shipyards of Messrs William Osborne who believe that where men's lives are at stake nothing but the best will do.

Selsey Bill lies about ten miles to the west of Littlehampton and in 1861 a lifeboat station was established there. In the R.N.L.I. Journal of 1st July, 1861 the following account appeared: "The National Lifeboat Institution has recently placed a lifeboat at Selsey, in Sussex, for the protection of the crews of vessels which get stranded on the Owers Banks and other shoals in the neighbourhood of Selsey Bill. Selsey being only a poor fishing village, a branch of the Institution has been formed at Chichester, to aid in supporting this establishment, with the title of the 'Chichester and West Sussex Branch of the National Lifeboat Institution'.* A double banked lifeboat, 35 foot long and rowing 12 oars, was forwarded to Chichester, together with a transporting carriage, on the 5th June, whence, after a public exhibition of some of her proportions, she was drawn to her station on her own carriage. The cost (£180) of this boat was presented to the Institution by some members of the Society of Friends."

Modern visitors to Selsey may find this description surprising. They would find it even more surprising to envisage a great stretch of park-land to the south and east of Selsey. In *Hills and the Sea* Hilaire Belloc wrote, "Through the park used to run a little dell known as the Looe stream and today this stream, right out at sea, furnishes the only gate by which ships can pass through the great maze of banks and rocks which go right out to sea from Selsey Bill, miles and miles, and are known as the Owers.

*Chichester Harbour also had a station from 1867-1884.

On the chart that district is still called 'The Park' and at very low tides stumps of the old trees can be seen . . ."

The Owers rocks have always been a danger to shipping and before ever a lightship was stationed here, beacon fires were lit on the headlands as a warning. It was not until 1788 that a lightship was moored to mark the place, and ever since that time the alternate red and white flashes have warned vessels away from the area. The lightship herself is about eleven miles off the coast, and about two miles from her is a most perilous spot where the rocks are covered by only a few feet of water which pours over them in the form of a "race".

The lifeboat, *The Friend*, was built by Forrestt and was a self-righter weighing 2 tons 15 cwt. A special lifeboat-house was put up for her at a cost of £19. After rescuing seven people from the brig *Governor Maclean* of London this boat was replaced by another bearing the same name, built by Woolfe in 1871. She was slightly smaller, 32 foot × 7½ foot pulling ten oars and after saving six people from the brig *Sarah Ann* of Jersey, was re-named *Four Sisters* continuing under her new name until 1885 in the course of which time she saved 49 lives. The problems of launching, which have always been a difficulty at Selsey with rapid coast erosion, began to show themselves during her spell here, the sea encroaching and threatening the lifeboat-house, so in 1874 it was decided to try keeping the boat afloat. This was the case when the *John and Henry Skynner*, ON 37, also built by Woolfe, came here. She was followed by the *Lucy Newbon*, ON 360, a larger 40 foot × 10 foot self-righter built by Forrestt which served until 1919.

One of the great services by Sussex lifeboats occurred during this time, when at about 7 p.m. on 31st August, 1908 the passengers and crew of the pleasure steamer *Queen* of Southampton, 120 of them in all, were on their way back from a day trip to Brighton. The weather was growing rougher, the wind piping up from the south-west and the captain, apparently fearing that the seas out in the Channel would be rather too much for his passengers, cut in-shore, making for the Looe stream. Unhappily he must have missed his bearings or the wind proved too strong for he struck on a bank. An hour or so later the rising tide and some furious manoeuvring with his engines brought the *Queen* clear but as she wallowed on her way in the increasing seas the steering gear broke. Helpless she drifted back across the reefs and the captain, afraid that she might go aground in an even worse position set off distress signals, issuing lifebelts to his passengers.

All this time Coxswain Sparshott at Selsey had been watching and as he saw the *Queen* off-course had assembled his men but when she seemed safely on her way he had dismissed them. They had not even reached their homes before the crack of the bursting rockets from the ship sent them hurrying back and they launched into the tumbling sea. Some fishermen and Coastguards had also launched and had managed to put pilot James Lawrence aboard the steamer. He at once told the captain where he could find good holding ground for his anchor and the *Queen* had brought up safely by the time the anxious passengers saw the blue and white form of the lifeboat battling towards them. Fascinated they watched her drop anchor and veer down in their direction, reeling about in the waves till ropes were flung and she was warped in alongside. Imagine the problems of first getting the women and children overside in such conditions, and in the twilight, to say nothing of the violent wind and rain. The leaping and falling lifeboat must have looked a puny craft to their frantic gaze as she ranged in on the wave crests, the lifeboatmen with outstretched arms catching the first batch of survivors, one by one, at just the right moment. When he had 30 aboard the coxswain decided not to take any more, so he told the captain he would land them, then come out again for more. By this time other boats were pulling out from the beach and the survivors were transhipped to them before the *Lucy Newbon* turned about and headed back for the *Queen*.

She was riding to her anchor safely, although pitching heavily in the scend of the seas, a motion tolerable for the crew but miserable for the wretched passengers who, huddled in the swamped saloon waited in acute anxiety. The captain now reckoned that the risk of transferring any more in the gathering darkness was too great so he and the coxswain agreed that the lifeboat should return ashore until daybreak. Throughout the night the lifeboatmen stood by on the beach while the gale continued to rage but towards morning it increased in violence and was soon blowing a hurricane. More signals came from the *Queen* and again the *Lucy Newbon* put off, tossing frenziedly in much worse conditions. Once more the coxswain veered down on his anchor cable, a rope was hurled and she was brought in alongside. More cold and frightened passengers were dragged into the lifeboat as she surged about, caught by a breaking crest she crunched heavily against the steamer's side splintering her gunwale, as she dropped sharply into a trough the rope twanged and snapped, the two ends whipping back like snakes. Although the lifeboatmen tried to veer in with a bridle, pulling with all their might at the starboard oars, a fierce eddy kept swirling her away. In the end the coxswain decided to lie to his anchor hoping for the hurricane to ease.

After two hours, however, with no let up in the weather and with 27 shivering survivors in the boat, he decided to set course for Littlehampton as it was hopeless now to attempt a landing at Selsey. Shortly afterwards naval tugs arrived on the scene and after some difficulty put a tow-line aboard the *Queen* and she was dragged to safety.

There was a rather moving sequel to this for thirty-six years later a Mrs Gilchrist of Birmingham, who had been a passenger on the *Queen*, left £200 to the R.N.L.I. and a further £200 to the surviving members of the 1908 lifeboat crew.

One of those who received a share in this legacy was Frederick Barnes, the rugged fisherman who was nicknamed "Rough Weather Barnes" by the *Sussex Daily News*, as he was second coxswain of the *Lucy Newbon* at the time. He reckoned that one of the worst gales he had ever known was the one on 6th December, 1929 when they went out to the *Honved* which, in the end, was able to get under way again after repairs to her engines. On that occasion the Selsey boat could not land because of the tremendous waves and had to ride out the storm till they had been 12 hours at sea. Fred Barnes had been coxswain of the first motor lifeboat stationed at Selsey, the *Jane Holland*, ON 673, built by Samuel White of Cowes, a 40 foot × 10 foot self-righter which had been concerned in the rescue of 11 lives in her spell of duty from 1922 to 1929. A new boathouse and slipway had been built shortly before her arrival so the problem of getting the boat away had been eased.

At the time of the *Honved* incident the new motor lifeboat *Canadian Pacific*, ON 714, had just arrived at the station. She was one of the first twin-engined 45½ foot × 12½ foot Watson's built by Saunders of Cowes the previous year, originally named *H. F. Bailey II* and allocated to Cromer. The Cromer crew were not happy with her and when their own *H. F. Bailey* was repaired, this boat, ON 714, was renamed *Canadian Pacific*. Fred Barnes was tremendously impressed by her and said, "She behaved so splendidly that I had little cause for anxiety," adding, "I would go round the world with her without any hesitation."

He had a chance to test her capabilities to the full on 2nd November, 1930 when a yacht, the *Lucy B* of Rye, got into trouble in a south-westerly gale on its way from Poole to Littlehampton. Some of the gear carried away, the engine would not start, and when the crew lowered their anchor it would not hold as the yacht snubbed at the cable in the steep seas that were running. When the *Canadian Pacific* launched at 10.30 a.m. she found the *Lucy B* already in the breakers not half a mile from the shore and the two men on board about to make a desperate bid for safety by swimming for it. Without a moment's hesitation the coxswain took the lifeboat right into the breakers, ran alongside and one of the men leapt to safety. At

Paddle steamer *Queen* of the Isle of Wight and South of England Royal Mail Steam Packet Co. Ltd.
From the collection of E. D. G. Payne

that moment the yacht slewed away, as she was caught by a breaker and Coxswain Barnes tried to swing alongside but again the yacht surged away. By this time both boats were right in the surf and the waves were breaking clean over the lifeboat. At times the smother of seas hid her completely from the watchers on the shore but handling her with wonderful skill the coxswain and his men managed to get a line aboard and, by breeches-buoy, were able to drag the other survivor through the surf to safety. The water was so shallow that the *Canadian Pacific* could not turn so she had to come out of it stern first, the cockpit filled by breakers several times but she got clear. Soon afterwards the yacht piled up on the beach.

This was not the end of the day for the lifeboatmen, and at 10.40 the same evening, still with the same monstrous seas running, the lifeboat was called out again. Fred Barnes and his men went plunging out into the wild night to fight their way for six miles to the Greek steamer *Menelaos*. Her steering gear had gone, her hatches were stove in and she was drifting helplessly towards the shoals. A Leyland liner had answered her S.O.S. and had taken off 12 of her crew but, because the *Menelaos* was so close to the shoals and the waves breaking over the rocks so enormous, she had to stand off at a safe distance. As the lifeboat reached the scene Coxswain Barnes realised that the remaining men must be taken off without delay before the steamer struck and foundered. It was a tricky job to run in alongside in the breaking seas but he achieved it and the survivors were soon clambering down a rope and being hauled aboard the *Canadian Pacific*. By 2 a.m. the lifeboat was back at Selsey and the Greek seamen were being cared for ashore.

For the rescue of the two men from the *Lucy B* Coxswain Barnes was awarded the bronze medal, and the Greek Government also awarded him a silver medal for the *Menelaos* service and a diploma to all the crew. It is interesting to note the names of the crew of the *Canadian Pacific* on these two launches as many old Selsey lifeboat families were represented:— George Arnell was second coxswain, A. Fullick was bowman, L. Phillips was mechanic, A. Pennicord, assistant mechanic, D. Grant, Signalman, S. Barnes, the coxswain's son, L. Pennicord and W. Millington. Leslie Pennicord became coxswain in 1936 and held that office until his retirement in 1952. The Chairman of the local branch at that time, Mr E. G. Arnell, J.P. had been in the Chair for twenty years and connected with the lifeboat service for fifty-seven, having been in the boat. The then Honorary Secretary, Mr R. T. Moger, was so keen on the lifeboat station that he was always to be found along the shore, talking with the fishermen and lifeboat crew. He also compiled a fascinating scrap-book which was presented to the Selsey station by his widow Mrs Nellie Moger and his daughter Mrs Cara Ashley in 1965.

Fred Barnes retired as coxswain in 1936 after a fine record with the boat. He had first joined the crew in 1902, was second coxswain in 1904 and became coxswain in 1917. He had been involved in the saving of 162 lives in the course of his years in the service.

The *Canadian Pacific* went off for overhaul in 1937 but was involved in a disastrous fire at the Cowes yard of Groves and Guttridge. The reserve boat *The*

Left: Fred Barnes of Selsey, coxswain of the first motor lifeboat at Selsey, a position he held from 1917-1956. *Right:* Coxswain D. Grant who won the silver medal for gallantry for his rescues from the *Maaslust, Coima* and *Bloodhound* in 1956.

Left: Family collection. Right: Chichester Photographic Service. R.N.L.I.

Brothers therefore took over until *Canadian Pacific II*, ON 803, built by Robertson and 46 foot × 12 foot 9 inches, could be placed on station. She served from 1938 to 1965 having the tremendous total of 286 launches during which 157 lives were saved.

In her many awards for gallantry were won. The Bronze Medal was awarded to Coxswain Leslie Pennicord in 1951 when the lifeboat stood by the motor vessel *Swift* of Costa Rica all night in one of those blustering south-westerly gales which kick up such a nasty sea off the Bill. Finally he succeeded in rescuing her crew of six after bringing the lifeboat alongside three times to enable the men to jump. For two days afterwards he was completely unable to see as a result of spray-blindness. The Maud Smith award for the bravest act of lifesaving for the year was given to W. Arnell in 1950 when he sprang overboard from the lifeboat to rescue a man who was trying to swim ashore from an overturned boat in a choppy sea. The Silver Medal was awarded to Coxswain D. Grant for his outstandingly skilful rescue of 18 people from the yachts *Maaslust, Coima* and *Bloodhound* right in among the rocks in appalling conditions of wind and sea on 29th July, 1956. With seas sweeping the decks Coxswain Grant held the lifeboat's bow up to *Bloodhound's* starboard side to take off seven men and two women; the 40 ton boeier *Maaslust* was a more difficult problem as the lee-boards prevented his coming alongside. He therefore drove the lifeboat's stem right on to the low bulwark and held it there with the engines while the three men, one woman and two children were hauled to safety. On his way to Portsmouth to land the survivors, the coxswain saw the six-metre *Coima* about to go go ashore and, coming up on her starboard quarter, rescued the crew just before she sank.

In 1958 work was begun on a new lifeboat station as coast erosion had been going on at the rate of 21 feet a year. The gangway to the old lifeboat-house had been extended and extended until it was over 270 yards in length. With a detailed programme of coast defence works undertaken by the West Sussex County Council the position seemed to have become more stabilised so it was considered feasible to build a new station on the foreshore with much better access. This work was completed in 1960 and the new lifeboat-house was duly opened by the Duke of Richmond and Gordon on 18th July, 1960.

During recent years there have been innumerable services to yachts in distress, to overturned boats and dinghies, but sometimes also to trawlers in difficulties through engine failure, as in the case of the Brixham trawler *Forseti* which was towed into Littlehampton after being aground near Selsey Bill in November 1958. Also sick men have been brought ashore from the Owers Lightship. However in 1963 a more serious incident occurred when on 4th January the Belgian trawler *Don Bosco* reported a fire in her engine-room.

With portable fire-fighting equipment and firemen from Selsey on board, the *Canadian Pacific II* set off, finding the casualty close to the Owers lightship, with smoke and flames licking the wheelhouse. A helicopter had already picked up three of the trawler's crew from a raft, two more were on board the lightship from which the lifeboat took them to Selsey. Meanwhile Admiralty fire-fighting tugs arrived on the scene and, when the fire was extinguished, took the vessel round to Portsmouth.

10th August, 1965 was a busy day and at about 10 a.m. the Coastguard sighted some red flares from a 45 foot boat that was towing a yacht. A helicopter was also "scrambled" and hovered over the casualty until the lifeboat drew near. The larger vessel, the ex-motor fishing vessel *Spectre* had broken down so both the boats were taken in tow and brought into Littlehampton. The *Canadian Pacific II* was back at her station by half-past three. Before the motor mechanic, who had been making his customary check of fuel and equipment could reach home his wife came hurrying to meet him with the message that there was a cargo ship on the rocks five miles east of Selsey Bill. The lifeboatmen went out again, this time finding a motor vessel, the *Ariel*, on the Outer Owers rocks with her radio was out of order and unable to send messages. The *Canadian Pacific II* stood by until the ship re-floated safely but was not back at her station till 10.35 p.m.

With the increasing number of services close in-shore it was decided to station an I.L.B. here in 1968 and in the first eight years of operation it has rescued 49 lives in the course of 122 calls.

After an exceedingly long spell of service, including 50 launches during the war, the *Canadian Pacific II* was withdrawn and a new Oakley self-righting type lifeboat was sent here in 1968, the *Charles Henry*, ON 1015. She was built by Osborne of Littlehampton, is 48½ foot × 14 foot, the finest and most modern type of lifeboat with all the latest equipment in the way of radar, echo sounders etc. Already she has been responsible for rescuing 35 lives bringing the total for the station to 309 in the course of which three Silver and two Bronze Medals have been won. In her, under Coxswain Bill Jones, there has been and will continue to be the same skilful seamanship and readiness to help which prompted old Fred Barnes to say at the time of the *Menelaos* presentation, "It is very nice of these people to say these kind words. We always do our best, you cannot do more than that. And there is no greater love than this: that a man lay down his life for his friend."

Citation and silver medal presented to the Selsey lifeboat for the service to the Greek steamer *Menelaos* in 1930.
Family collection

Silver Medal and Diploma presented to the Selsey Life-boat by the Greek Government in recognition of services rendered to S.S. "Menelaos" 2nd November 1930.

CHAPTER TEN

WARTIME SERVICES

NO HISTORY of the Kent and Sussex Lifeboat Stations would be complete without a reference to the notable deeds performed when to the perils of the sea were added the threat of minefields, bombs and aerial machine-gun attacks.

In both World Wars many of the lifeboatmen were away, serving in the Royal Naval Reserve, and the crews had to be made up with retired lifeboatmen or service personnel home on leave. But true to Sir William Hillary's principles, the boats were launched for "the preservation of human life from shipwreck, help to ships in distress, the succour and support of the rescued regardless of nationality". The weekly average of lives saved in the First World War was 18; in the Second World War it was 21.

The Eastbourne lifeboat *James Stevens No 6* joined the Newhaven boat *Sir Fitzroy Clayton* in going to the aid of the Cunarder *Alaunia** on 19th October, 1916 after she had been damaged either by a mine or, more likely, a torpedo in the vicinity of the Royal Sovereign lightship. One of the fast patrol boats of the Dover Patrol was first on the scene, taking off 20 people from the liner, then putting one of her own officers and seven naval ratings aboard in the hope of beaching the severely damaged ship. However, they were beaten by the weather and were forced to abandon her, clambering aboard the *James Stevens* while the Newhaven boat landed a further six as well as the 20 survivors from the patrol boat.

Minefields posed an even greater threat in the Second World War, and not only enemy mines. Off Dover a patrolling trawler, the *Blackburn Rovers*, was on watch for submarines near a deep mine-field when her propeller was seized up by a wire rope. All efforts to free it proved unavailing so her captain anchored. The anchor started to drag and the November gale swept the trawler toward the mine-field, the anchor and cable likely at any moment to detonate one of them. Dover lifeboat launched to her assistance, Coxswain Colin Bryant and crew well aware of the danger, even though they had the Assistant King's harbour-master on board with a chart of the mine-field, for beyond the deep one was a zone of shallow mines towards which the trawler was being driven remorselessly. The crew of the *Blackburn Rovers* had almost given up hope when the lifeboat *Sir William Hillary* hove in sight but before they could be rescued all the secret papers and mine-detecting gear must be transferred and time fuses lit to send the ship to the bottom.

While the two boats drifted through the deep mine-field, drawing steadily nearer to the shallow one, the waves tossed them about so violently that more than once they crashed together. As they rose and fell every man there knew that the next trough might bring a shattering explosion. After a nerve-tingling delay all the gear

*The *Alaunia* was a small Cunard vessel on the Canadian run which had dropped most of her passengers at Plymouth prior to this incident.

Left: Coxswain Howard Primrose Knight of Ramsgate. Awarded D.S.M. for "gallantry and determination" in bringing off 2,800 men of the B.E.F. at Dunkirk. *Right:* Coxswain Edward Drake Parker of Margate. Awarded D.S.M. for "gallantry and determination" at Dunkirk.   *R.N.L.I.*

was safely transferred, the 16 men from the trawler came tumbling aboard and the Dover lifeboat ploughed out of this peril to face a hard slog back to harbour.

Nor was it only sea mines that presented such a risk. With the threat of invasion after Dunkirk desperate measures were taken all along the coast. Gaps were blown in piers—fortunately the one at Margate was to seaward of the lifeboat-house, for Margate was one of the busiest stations during the Battle of Britain. Barbed-wire entanglements and land-mines festooned the beaches, so that the Eastbourne lifeboat, for example, could not launch. The Navy intervened but only after four months was a way cleared for her. At Dungeness even the slipway was treated to an immense barbed-wire entanglement while land-mines were buried everywhere in the shingle. Here again the Navy insisted that whatever else was done in the way of defensive work, the lifeboat must be free to launch. At Selsey the land-mines in the beach were constantly exposed by coast erosion. No-one knew when a wave might strike one of them and set it off; everyone on his way to the lifeboat-house was in deadly peril.

All these anti-invasion measures came into force after those memorable days at the end of May and beginning of June 1940 when 350,000 troops were brought off safely from the exposed beaches of Dunkirk owing their lives to the fleet of small craft, quickly mobilised, which carried out their appointed task so nobly in the face of every kind of danger.

As soon as the R.N.L.I. received a call for boats from the Ministry of Shipping it telephoned the eighteen stations from Gorleston to Shoreham Harbour asking them to send their boats at once to Dover for special duty under the Admiralty.

Before other boats could leave, however, the naval officers at Margate and Ramsgate asked those boats to go. The *Prudential* of Ramsgate under Coxswain Howard Primrose Knight was first away, towing eight wherries, long shallow rowing-boats, behind her, and with an additional party of 18 naval ratings to supplement her crew. By about eight in the evening she reached Dunkirk where heavy black smoke from the burning port stung the eyes, then went on to Malo Les Bains. As soon as it was dark the wherries were sent in to fetch off the troops. Three of these boats manned by naval ratings must have missed their way for they were not seen again. The remaining three manned by lifeboatmen plus another manned by ratings worked on throughout the night, making contact in pitch darkness with the officers ashore, taking troops aboard and pulling out with them to the lifeboat.

As one of these wherries came in, a voice called out of the night, "I cannot see who you are. Are you a naval party?"

"No, sir — men of the Ramsgate lifeboat."

The voice called back, "Thank you, and thank God for such men as you have proved yourselves to be. There is a party of 50 Highlanders coming now."

In this way all through the night the men toiled on, bringing in the wherries stern first, waiting while the soldiers clambered in, then pulling out to the lifeboat. By daybreak some 800 men had been ferried off and, as the *Prudential* could only take 160, she in turn had transhipped them to a motor-ship lying further off-shore.

As day dawned enemy action increased, so did the wind. A nasty surf was beginning to break, boats capsized, but more and more troops were streaming on to the beach. With wreckage floating everywhere the lifeboatmen found it impossible to row the wherries so, instead, they were floated in from the lifeboat lying about 80 yards off-shore, then hauled out again, the soldiers using their tin-hats as bailers. Still the troops flowed down the beach in a never ending stream, wading out at their officers' orders and climbing into the wherries without rush or scramble.

At length the lifeboat was asked to move eastward to La Panne with the three remaining wherries. All through the Friday afternoon and evening the crew worked on, helping to tow small boats, hauling out the wherries till the last of them was smashed by shell-fire. At 1.30 on Saturday morning, the crew utterly exhausted, the wherries gone, the lifeboat headed for Ramsgate. For forty hours in all she had been out, for thirty of them working off the beaches under constant fire, and she and her gallant crew had helped to bring off 2,800 men.

The Margate lifeboat *Lord Southborough* meanwhile had sailed somewhat later under Coxswain Edward Drake Parker, in tow of a Dutch yacht, arriving off Nieuport where conditions on the beach were even more difficult. However again and again she worked in as close as she could to the beach on her anchor cable,

Pilot Officer Richard Hillary, rescued by Margate life-boat, 3rd September, 1940. He was of the family of R.N.L.I. founder, Sir William Hillary.   *R.N.L.I.*

picking up a full load of men for transfer to the yacht. When this craft was fully loaded she plied between the shore and the destroyer H.M.S. *Icarus*, running the gauntlet of dive-bombing from J U 88s and bursts of machine-gun fire. The swell increased all the time and at length she could no longer work close in. Instead she ranged to and fro outside the surf to rescue those who had put off in wrecked boats or rafts. She saved many in this way.

At last wind and surf made it impossible to do more, so she headed back for Margate, having been out for nearly 24 hours and saving some 600 men.

Both these boats had much work to do at their own stations for many of the last troops to leave the beaches were on rafts, in small boats, or in damaged craft. Boats full of soldiers were found drifting around near the Goodwins, motor craft were adrift with ropes round their propellers; and there were also the normal dangers of fog and collision with such a mass of small craft on the move.

Both the Coxswains, Howard Primrose Knight and Edward Drake Parker, were awarded the Distinguished Service Medal for their gallantry and determination and the flag of the R.N.L.I. that had flown at the mast-head of the *Prudential* throughout the service now hangs in St George's Parish Church in Ramsgate.

Such was the part played by Margate and Ramsgate in those heroic days, but what of the other Kent and Sussex boats? Their story is not so well known for in the rush of mobilising every available small craft misunderstandings arose and the Navy took over the lifeboats as they arrived at Dover which was the headquarters of the whole operation. In due course Dungeness arrived back off Margate with four

Reserve lifeboat *J. B. Proudfoot* on duty at Margate. This was the crew and the boat that picked up Richard Hillary.   *R.N.L.I.*

sailors aboard, one of them wounded, and with two of her stanchions torn away. Walmer returned with shell-holes through both sides — but, being a lifeboat, did not sink. The Dover boat was in service with the Navy and the former Lowestoft boat which was at the station in reserve saved 50. Hastings returned with one of her end-boxes damaged. Eastbourne was taken across by a Naval officer who later reported what had happened: she had first been rammed by a French destroyer, then sprayed with machine-gun fire by a German Messerschmitt, and finally he had to abandon her when she came under heavy shell-fire. Two days later she was found drifting in the Channel and was brought in to Dover, her fore end-box stove in, 500 bullet holes in her sides, water washing about in the damaged hull. But she did not sink. She was repaired but it was not until April 1941 that she was able to return to her station. Of all the 19 lifeboats at Dunkirk only the Hythe boat, *Viscountess Wakefield*, was lost.

To round off the story of this heroic service mention should be made of the Navy's appreciation. All through the evacuation Commander J. M. Upton, the Inspector of Lifeboats for the East Coast district, and some of the Institution's mechanics had been working night and day to service and maintain all the miscellaneous motor-craft, not only lifeboats, that had been operating out of Dover. At the end of the operation the Admiral Commanding wrote to Commander Upton of his deep gratitude to him and his men for their invaluable help. The

164

Commander of the destroyer H.M.S. *Icarus* said, "The magnificent behaviour of the crew of the Margate lifeboat who, with no thought of rest, brought off load after load of soldiers from Dunkirk under continuous shelling, bombing and aerial machine-gun fire will be an inspiration to us as long as we live."

During the Battle of Britain, as was mentioned earlier, Margate was one of the busiest lifeboat stations. It was strangely appropriate that, on 3rd September, 1940 when the reserve lifeboat *J. B. Proudfoot* was on duty here, the crew put to sea to rescue a badly burned young fighter pilot who had baled out over the Thames Estuary. He was just on the point of drowning when at last they located him and when he was landed at Margate they learned that he was Pilot Officer Richard Hillary, great-great-great nephew of the founder of the R.N.L.I.

The toughness and endurance of the lifeboats was matched by the toughness and endurance of the men. In 1943 there was another astonishing example of these qualities at Newhaven. A naval trawler, the *Avanturine*, was reported to be in difficulties off Cuckmere Haven on a dark December night with squalls of rain and a gale from the south-west. The Newhaven lifeboat *Cecil and Lilian Philpott* set out into the darkness under Coxswain Leonard Peddlesden, finding the trawler only about 500 yards off the shore, close in to a reef. The shore batteries were playing their lights on her, the trawler was letting off flares and in the alternating glare between brilliant light and inky darkness the lifeboatmen made out that the *Avanturine* was at anchor for there was a hawser over her bows. The coxswain lowered

Walmer lifeboat *Charles Dibdin Civil Service No. 2* coming ashore during the war. Convoy of ships in the "Downs" in background.
R.N.L.I.

his anchor and, paying out his cable, took the lifeboat carefully stern first toward the casualty. Suddenly he saw the trawler's bows on the top of the next crest, coming straight at him. He put his engines hard astern but a huge wave flung the lifeboat right at those advancing bows. They cut deep into the hull, making a great hole in the deck, the mast shattered into three pieces crashing down among the crew and bringing the wireless aerial with it. All the crew except for the two motor mechanics were hurled to the deck by the impact, the coxswain was flung against the steering-rod pitching right over it, the second coxswain was struck across the face and was only saved from going overboard by the buckle of his lifejacket catching in a cleat. In the darkness and confusion Coxswain Peddlesden did not know the extent of the damage, only that the boat was becoming more and more difficult to handle. Crippled with pain he took the boat out to his anchor while the crew set about clearing the wreckage. At that moment another huge sea came at them, the damaged lifeboat could not rise to it and, when it had passed, the bowman, Ben Clarke, had been swept away.

The captain of the trawler had seen nothing of the lifeboat till the shock of the collision flung down one of his crew. At once he went astern and lowered anchor. His helm was jammed so the only way he could claw off the shore was by steaming in a series of half-circles, then anchoring again till the trawler's bows swung into position for another half-circle. In this laborious way he crept away from danger, the damaged lifeboat escorting him till the *Avanturine* was safe.

Even then the coxswain did not make for shore but stood by for over half-an-hour in case any other vessel should need help in reaching harbour. When at last the day came the full extent of the damage to the boat could be seen. The trawler's bows had cut two foot deep into her, making a great gash 2½ foot across through which the seas had been surging into the petrol compartment, the petrol tank had been struck so hard that it had a waist to it like an hour-glass, had been torn off its stand and had fractured a bulkhead. But all the time it had not even sprung a leak and had continued to supply the engine through its twisted feed pipe.

These are only a few of the services rendered by lifeboats during those dark days of war but they serve to show, as nothing else can, the strength of the boats themselves and the spirit of their crews, who risked their lives for the ideal so well summed up by Lord Mottistone, himself a lifeboatman, many years ago: "The intense joy of the thing achieved, when the rescued men are safely on board, is about the most wonderful thing in human experience."

Glossary

Aback	The situation of the sails when the wind blows on the wrong side of sail, thus bringing the boat to a sudden halt or forcing it astern.
Anchor fluke	The triangular plates at the extremity of an arm of an anchor, terminating in a point called the bill.
Athwart	Across.
Barge	Flat bottomed coastal trader with lee-boards each side to prevent the vessel making leeway. A spritsail barge has the peak of mainsail held up by a long spar from foot of mast called a sprit.
Barque or Bark	Sailing vessel square-rigged on all masts except the last, which is fore- and aft-rigged.
Batten down	Close and secure openings, especially in the deck, of a vessel.
Beam ends	A boat is said to be "on her beam ends" when she is heeled over so far that her deck beams are practically vertical.
Beat	Sail against the wind by tacking to and fro across the wind.
Beaufort Scale	Admiral Sir Francis Beaufort (1774-1857) devised a scale of wind forces which was generally adopted and has been in use ever since.

Beaufort Scale Force	Nautical m.p.h.	Description and sea conditions
0	0-1	Calm — flat calm
1	1-3	Light airs — small wavelets
2	4-6	Light breeze — small waves, crests not breaking
3	7-10	Gentle breeze — large wavelets, crests beginning to break
4	11-16	Moderate breeze — small waves, longer crests breaking
5	17-21	Fresh breeze — moderate waves, crests breaking
6	22-27	Strong breeze — large waves, crests breaking
7	28-33	Near gale — foam-streaked large waves
8	34-40	Gale — high waves, spindrift from crests
9	41-47	Strong gale — high waves, foam, crests roll over
10	48-55	Storm — very high waves, overhanging crests, much white foam
11	56-65	Violent storm — exceptionally high waves, foam everywhere
12	above 65	Hurricane — air filled with spray visibility badly affected

Bend	To make fast, join.
Boeier	A type of Dutch barge-yacht with lee-boards. In high seas lee-boards tend to bang about forming an obstruction which can prevent a vessel or lifeboat from coming alongside.
Bowman	A very responsible position in the lifeboat. Stationed in the bows to handle ropes, secure lifeboat alongside other boats, keep a look-out, etc.
Breeches-buoy	A lifebelt with canvas breeches in which the rescued can sit safely while the belt is hauled, by rope and tackle, to the rescuers.

Bridle	Rope attached between anchor cable and some part of the boat to swing her to the desired angle.
Brig	A two-masted vessel, square-rigged on both masts.
Broached to	Swung suddenly broadside to the wind.
Cinque Ports	It was the duty of these ports to supply ships for the King in time of war, until Tudor times, in exchange for certain rights and privileges. They are still proud of their historical associations. They were:

Cinque Ports	Limbs
Hastings	Pevensey, Seaford
Romney	Lydd
Hythe	
Dover	Folkestone, Faversham, Margate, St Peters
Sandwich	Fordwich, Deal, Walmer, Ramsgate, Sarre, Brightlingsea (Essex)

Plus two

Ancient towns	
Rye	Tenterden
Winchelsea	

Coxswain	Skipper of the lifeboat. In Waveney type boats he is skipper and mechanic.
Cranky	Likely to behave in an awkward, unexpected and unhandy manner; dangerous.
Dead reckoning	Estimation of position when astronomical observation and fixing by cross bearings are not possible. Normally by course and distance run from last known position with allowance made for leeway, currents etc.
Dolphin-striker	A short perpendicular spar under the bowsprit for guying down the wire stay under the bowsprit.
Drogue	A cone shaped bag towed behind a boat to slow her and prevent the waves causing her to broach, to keep her on a straight line when approaching the shore and preventing her turning broadside to the beach.
Fathom	Six feet.
Fore-end box	The front decked-in part of the lifeboat.
Foying	Local term for supplying victuals etc.
Galley punts	Small 21 to 30 foot sailing craft with lug sail, approximately amidships, carrying a crew of three or four
Gig	Small ship's boat, used for going ashore.
Gybe	Wind catching the other side of the mainsail causing it to set on the opposite side. If involuntary or uncontrolled in a heavy wind this can be very dangerous. Normally occurs when a sailing vessel is running before the wind.
Halyards	Ropes to haul up yards or sails.
Haul off warp	Stout hawser attached to an anchor laid off-shore the other end brought in and made fast ashore. Used to assist launching.
Hoveller	A seaman whose trade was hovelling or supplying ships with whatever was needed — chandlery, victuals, etc.
Hoy	In England, as opposed to Holland, a Hoy was a single masted vessel with a fore-and-aft sail of up to 60 tons. They were coastal vessels generally carrying passengers between ports (e.g. the Margate Hoy with passengers between Margate and London) or such things as supplies (e.g. Naval Hoys provisioning warships).
Jury rig	Temporary makeshift mast and sails rigged after vessel disabled.
Kedge anchor	Spare or reserve anchor usually lighter than the main one.
Ketch	Two-masted vessel fore-and-aft rigged on both masts, the mizzen being smaller than the main.

Leeward	Down wind, thus the leeward side provides protection from the wind for any boat coming alongside.
Limb	See Cinque Ports.
Luff	Bring the ship's head closer to the wind.
Luggers	Big boats, often 40 foot by 13 foot, with two masts carrying lugsails. They had little cabin space but usually some forward shelter.
Missing stays	Failing to come round on to the other tack.
Reef, to	To shorten sail. Sails usually had three sets of reef-points except square sails which usually had two. The amount the sail was shortened was determined by which set was used.
R.N.R.	Royal Naval Reserve, originally officers and men of the Merchant Navy who volunteered to serve with the Royal Navy in wartime. In 1956 all naval reserves, including the Royal Naval Volunteer Reserve, were absorbed into the R.N.R. and all now use the same badges of rank as the Royal Navy.
Rubbing-strake	Cork, rubber or wood below gunwale to act as permanent fender. Usually painted red on a lifeboat.
Scend	Rise and fall of the sea in rough weather.
Schooner	A vessel fore-and-aft rigged on two or more masts sometimes with square topsails on her fore mast.
Smother	Local term used to denote scud and foam having no buoyancy.
Sponsons	In paddle-steamers they are part of the ship projecting either side of the paddle-wheels to support and protect the paddle-boxes.
Spritsails	Sails held up by a spar or sprit from base of mast to peak of sail.
Strand, to	To go aground.
Swatchways	Narrow tidal channels through sand and mud banks.
Thwarts	Seats fixed across the boat.
Transom	Piece of timber across the sternpost and bolted to it.
Trot boat	Boats to ferry crews out to vessels on moorings or trots.
Veer down	Allow boat to drop back, carried by wind and/or sea, whilst attached to a rope or anchor cable.
Veer (of wind)	Wind veers when it changes direction clockwise. When anti-clockwise it is said to back.
Yawing	Swinging about from side to side.

Metrication — Basic Conversions

1 foot = 0.3048 metres   1 metre = 3.280848 feet
1 inch = 2.540 centimetres   1 centimetre = 0.393701 inches

Money

Prior to decimalisation there were 240 pence or 20 shillings to one pound sterling. Thus the new ten pence piece is the equivalent of 2 shillings or 24 old pence in the old money.

Select Bibliography

Broadstairs, Past and Present, P. W. Barlow, 1882.
The Lifeboat Service, Oliver Warner, Cassell, 1974.
The Lifeboat Story, Patrick Howarth, Routledge, 1957.
Kent History Illustrated, F. W. Jessup, 1966, Kent Education Committee.
Launch, Major-General J. E. B. Seely, Hodder & Stoughton, 1932.
Memorials of the Goodwin Sands, G. B. Gattie, 1890.
Heroes of the Goodwin Sands, T. S. Treanor, RTS, 1904.
The Cinque Ports, R. F. & F. W. Jessup, Batsford, 1952.
Story of Broadstairs & St Peters, James Bird, Lane's, 1974.
Saved from the Sea, Robert Malster, Terence Dalton, 1974.
Pocket Pilot for the South Coast, Adlard Coles, Faber, 1950.
Life of Nelson, Southey, Dent's Everyman, 1906.
This England, W. S. Shears, RBC, 1937.
Forgotten Ports of England, George Goldsmith Carter, Evans, 1951.
Henry Blogg, Cyril Jolly, Harrap, 1958.
History of Deal, E. C. Pain.
Storm on the Waters, Charles Vince, Hodder & Stoughton, 1946.
Wreck & Rescue in the Bristol Channel, Grahame Farr, Barton, 1966.
Picture of Margate, Oulton, 1820.
Our English Watering Place, Charles Dickens, 1858.
Kent, Teignmouth Shore, A & C Black, 1907.
Sussex, R. F. Jessup, Methuen & Batsford, 1949.
Goodwin Sands Shipwrecks, R. Larne, David & Charles, 1977.
Discovering Lifeboats, E. W. Middleton, Shire Publications, 1972.
The Way of a Ship, Alan Villiers, Hodder & Stoughton, 1954.
Cinque Ports Country, John Huddlestone, Granville Publishing Co.
A Broad Place, W. H. Lapthome.
Ships Illustrated, Ian Allan.

Periodicals, Newspapers etc.

Kent Life
Sea Breezes
Illustrated London News
The Lifeboat, Journal of the R.N.L.I.
East Kent Mercury
Kent Messenger
East Kent Times
Morning Post
The Guardian
Pulleyn's *Kent Argus*
Keeble's *Margate and Ramsgate Gazette*
South Coast Mercury

Brighton and Hove Herald
Evening Argus
West Sussex Gazette
Chichester Post
Isle of Wight Observer
Isle of Wight County Press
Station histories: —
    Eastbourne
    Littlehampton
    Newhaven
    Rye
    Shoreham Harbour

Index

Lifeboats and Vessels Index

52 foot **Barnett**

48 foot 6 inch **Oakley**

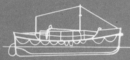

37 foot **Oakley**

OFFSHORE LIFEBOATS

47 foot **Watson**

46 foot 9 inch **Watson**

46 foot **Watson**

37 foot 6 inch **Rother**

42 foot **Watson**

48 foot 6 inch **Solent**

41 foot **Watson**

44 foot **Waveney**

Selsey § † ∘

Littlehampton †

Worthing ∘

Shoreham Harbour § †

Brighton

Newhaven §

Eas

ENGLISH CHANNEL